ONE DAY IN THE LIFE OF 179212

ONE DAY IN THE LIFE OF 179212

Notes from an American Prison

Jens Soering

Lantern Books • New York

A Division of Booklight Inc.

Lantern Books
128 Second Place
Brooklyn, NY 11231

www.lanternbooks.com

Copyright © 2012 Jens Soering

pbk ISBN: 978-1-59056-345-8

e ISBN: 978-1-59056-342-7

Library of Congress Cataloging-in-Publication Data

Söring, Jens, 1966–
[Tag im Leben des 179212. English]
One day in the life of 179212: notes from an
american prison / Jens Soering.
p. cm.
ISBN 978-1-59056-345-8 (pbk. : alk. paper) —
ISBN 978-1-59056-342-7 (ebook)
1. Söring, Jens, 1966– 2. Prisoners—Virginia—Biography.
3. Brunswick Correctional Center (Va.) 4. Murder—Virginia—
Lynchburg. 5. Trials (Murder)—Virginia. I. Title.
HV9468.S72A3 2012
365'.6092—dc23
[B]
2012000740

PREFACE

One Day in the Life of 179212 is an adaptation of *Ein Tag im Leben des 179212* written by Jens Soering and published by Gütersloher Verlagshaus in Germany in 2008. The book provides an hour-by-hour survey of everyday life in a medium-security prison in Virginia and an at times mordantly funny look at the prison-industrial complex.

One Day in the Life of 179212 is the fourth book by Jens that Lantern has published, after *The Way of the Prisoner, An Expensive Way to Make Bad People Worse*, and *The Church of the Second Chance*. As with his other work, Jens doesn't rehearse the details of the notorious double murder that led to his spending his entire adult life in prison. The case is outlined in Patricia McGinty's afterword to this book and described on Jens' website (www.jenssoering.com). *One Day*'s purpose is to illuminate the daily lives of human beings whom we've disposed of and forgotten about, to expose the twisted logic and inherent corruption that have warped the system whereby we dispense punishment, and to show how meditation and faith can release all of us from bondage.

In some ways, Jens' life has changed dramatically since *Ein Tag im Leben des 179212* was published in 2008. In 2009, Jens was moved from Brunswick Correctional Facility to another institution eighty miles to the north, where he is now prisoner 1161655. As Jens' newly written postscript to this book makes clear, his case has also taken a number of dramatic turns that couldn't have been foreseen when he completed the manuscript in 2007.

In other ways, however, the daily conditions of life in prison remain substantially the same—not simply for Jens, but for the 2.38 million men and women who continue to be confined in a capricious and inhumane system. Some of these people have committed terrible crimes and are a threat to public safety. But, as Jens shows, too many of the incarcerated suffer from mental illness or drug addiction, or are illiterate and/or learning-disabled, or are so old and sick that they belong in hospital or deserve compassionate release.

As Jens points out, there are occasional glimmers of hope: for instance, against all odds, the prisoner called Liam in *One Day* finally achieved parole. (All names in this book have been changed to protect prisoners' identities.) But as Jens' work illustrates in shocking detail, the politicization of criminal justice and the bizarre economic incentives built into the prison-industrial complex continue to corrode our society.

—Martin Rowe, Publisher, Lantern Books
December 22, 2011

4:20 A.M.

Every morning at twenty past four I wake up to the sound of the toilet flushing. The flush of a prison toilet is especially powerful, and therefore loud, because inmates use toilets to dispose of all kinds of things: trash, food scraps, torn bed linen, drugs, plastic bags used for brewing mash, and so on. In order to ensure that all the detritus disappears down the pipes, the guards turn up the water pressure as high as possible. Problem-free waste disposal is, after all, the primary mission of today's correctional system.

After flushing the toilet, my cell partner leaves for the day-room to watch TV. I climb down from the top bunk, make my bed, wash my face, brush my teeth, and pee—all in the dark. I don't need any light for my morning ritual because I've lived in this same cell for several years. There's not an inch of it I don't know by heart.

From the door to the barred window the cell measures eleven feet, six inches. The back half is six feet, eight inches wide, while the front is only five feet, four inches due to the pipe chase. Inside is the bunk bed, a wall-mounted table, a gray plastic chair, four metal lockers, two shelves, a sink, and a toilet. When my cell partner and I are both up and about, I have to press myself against the wall to allow him to go from the bed to the sink.

At this hour, however, I am alone and able to sit in the gray plastic chair to meditate. I do this three times a day, thirty-five to forty minutes at a time, for a total of about two hours. I began this practice in January 2000 while I was still at Wallens Ridge State Prison, at that time one of Virginia's two supermax facilities.

During the eleven months I spent at Wallens Ridge, I witnessed almost every abuse you can imagine and might even expect at such a place. Mentally ill prisoners howled out their misery; guards beat an inmate so badly that his blood spattered waist-high on the walls; two prisoners died under dubious circumstances; and hysterically barking dogs sometimes escorted us to and from the shower. Shootings were constant, even in the showers and the dining hall.

I was shot once, although it was unintentional, and I was only hit with a rubber pellet. A prisoner who'd just arrived and hadn't yet become accustomed to the rules of the supermax had gone to empty his rubbish into the large, gray trash can in the dayroom. The guard in the elevated gun port had screamed at him: Was he blind? Couldn't he see the red line on the floor around the trash can? That meant the prisoner had to ask permission before crossing it to throw away his trash. Everyone knew that!

The new inmate responded with a single expletive—not even an especially egregious one by prison standards—but it was enough to provoke the guard into firing a warning shot. It was a dummy round, but came with an incredibly loud BANG that bounced back and forth off the concrete walls of the dayroom. We old-timers threw ourselves to the floor; this kind of thing was almost routine by now. But the new prisoner remained on his feet, slightly crouched, looking from side to side in confusion. I was lifting my head to look around when the guard fired a live round at him, throwing the prisoner to the ground.

Like a swarm of angry bees, the marble-sized, hard rubber balls ricocheted off the floor and walls near the new inmate. One of them struck me on the left bicep. My face was near my upper arm because I was prone on the floor, so the hard rubber ball just missed my eye. A couple of inches in the wrong direction, and I could very well have been blinded. As it was, I wasn't injured physically, but the incident certainly left a psychological scar. In the following weeks, the slightest noise startled me deeply. And for some reason, I also became extremely nervous every time I had to pee.

Such unease was nothing compared to what the prisoner next to the trash can experienced. He was hit by the full force of many rubber pellets fired by the shotgun, and he was subjected to the therapeutic beating that the guards administered to any inmate whose actions provoked the use of firepower. Lots of reports have to be written and reviewed every time a weapon is fired, so *someone* has to pay for creating all that extra work.

As it turned out, the rubber ball that hit me in the arm was a blessing. I immediately filed a written complaint, reminded everyone that my father was a German diplomat (at the time, the *chargé d'affaires* in Papua New Guinea), and wrote angry letters describing the incident to the German Embassy in Washington, D.C. My efforts must have had some effect, for two months later I was transferred to Brunswick Correctional Center, the Commonwealth of Virginia's model prison. Every luxury the convict's heart desires can be found here—except freedom and hope.

In addition to my transfer to Brunswick, another positive and unexpected outcome of my stay at Wallens Ridge was that I began to meditate regularly. I did this to try to get away from a horrible reality. Although the wish to escape in my mind was part of the reason for beginning the practice, it certainly did not end up as the totality of it.

When I meditate, I am in touch with the Eternal, the Good, and the True. One can search for this trinity in the world beyond prison, too, but it's easy to be fooled into accepting substitutes. Instead of the truly Eternal, one might make do with a whole series of "eternal" loves. Instead of the genuinely Good, one may rely on one's Platinum MasterCard® to pursue the "American Dream." Instead of the really True, one might be satisfied with the many truths of our multicultural, global society. None of these are necessarily wrong in themselves, but each is only an image, a reflection of essence, and not the essence itself.

In the world of the penitentiary, however, there is no opportunity to confuse image with essence. Nothing in my world can possibly give the illusion of being the Eternal, the Good, and the True. There are diversions—"situational" homosexual activity, drugs, mash, and so forth—but not even we inmates are foolish enough to mistake these distractions for the real thing.

Fortunately, that Real Thing can be found—not in the outer reality, however, but in the inner world that I reach through meditation. In this inner world, I come to know the Eternal, the Good, and the True, and they give me the strength and courage to endure the daily trials of my outer world. I learned this at Wallens Ridge, which is why I can honestly say that, for me, the supermax was a blessing.

5:10 A.M.

At ten past five my first meditation session of the day ends. I go to the dayroom, and my cell partner gets to spend the next fifty minutes by himself in our "house."

This period of privacy is incredibly important, because in prison you're forced to spend the whole day with people you either don't know or don't like. You're constantly lonely, but never alone! Spending fifty minutes by yourself in the cell, without having to experience the presence of another person, is a genuine luxury.

I call the cell our "house," but the word "coffin" would be more apt. My cell partner and I "fell" (prison slang for being arrested) in 1982 and 1986 respectively. We're serving double-life sentences, so we'll almost certainly never be released. There are roughly 130,000 lifers in the U.S., and nearly all of us will die behind bars.[1]

While my cell partner enjoys his time alone, I sit at my regular table in the dayroom. It's relatively quiet at this time of day. Apart from a female guard dozing in her corner, there are only four or five others present, all diabetics waiting to take their insulin. Everyone stares at the large color television in the room.

The television is the most effective instrument of control known to modern corrections. Ever since TVs were installed in every penitentiary dayroom in the nation, the number of prison riots has fallen dramatically. Who has the will to fight for freedom or better living conditions if doing so means missing the latest rap video on Black Entertainment Television, or BET®?

In the outside world, and especially among African-Americans concerned about what their children are being exposed to, BET® has been subject to intense criticism for its glorification of the gangsta lifestyle and its misogynistic message. That criticism makes BET® unbelievably popular in prison, where almost everyone has some connection to the drug trade and where women are objects of fantasy rather than real human beings. Rap is the inescapable background music of penitentiary life. Wherever you go, no matter what time of day, you are always within reach of a radio or television spewing out this poison.

BET® is a classic example of what I call *correctional irony*. On the one hand, prison administrators find it much more efficient to control inmates with color televisions playing music videos than to hire more guards. On the other, the eventual reintegration of prisoners into society is made more difficult when they've been living on a diet of pure gangsta rap. After spending year upon year hypnotized by BET®, can you dream of any future other than becoming the biggest cocaine dealer of them all?

I will return to correctional irony many times in these pages. In each instance, the central paradox is the same: the very thing essential to the smooth and secure operation of the prison *also* makes rehabilitation impossible and destroys any vestige of morality that prisoners might still possess. The question I ask in response to that irony is fundamental to anyone concerned about the uses and abuses of imprisonment: If correctional facilities end up corrupting (or corrupting further) instead of correcting their charges, what is the point of the exercise?

The question is moot to the diabetics watching the dayroom TV. They'll never leave the penitentiary because they're lifers like me, and they're so old that they too despise BET® and refuse to drink the correctional Kool-Aid® of gangsta rap propaganda. At this hour, their favorite TV program is the local news from Virginia's capital, Richmond. Exterior shots of accident scenes or house fires often show these prisoners' old neighborhoods, providing them with an opportunity to see what their former haunts look like today, two or three decades after their involuntary departure. Every once in a while one of the diabetics murmurs, "Man, that corner there, I know that place! Back in the day I used to. . . ."

One of the homesick old-timers usually turns down the volume on the news, so I can read my German Bible without having to mentally filter out the English I might otherwise hear from the television. Since 1996, when all foreign language material was forbidden in the Virginia Department of Corrections, my Bible has been the only text in my native tongue to which I've had regular access. Other books, magazines, or newspapers in German—even reputable and well-known titles—have been *verboten*. They might contain something about prison breaks or terrorism.

When the prohibition was implemented, the German Embassy attempted to persuade the Department of Corrections that the books and periodicals I wanted weren't dangerous or subversive. However, the administrators weren't particularly interested that a German inmate might wish to stay in touch with his language and culture, much like the diabetics who watch the local TV news. As far as the correctional system is concerned, I'm in prison solely to be punished.

As a result of the lack of reading material, my German vocabulary has shrunk to terms found in my Bible. I can still understand "sin," "repentance," "mercy," and "love" in my mother tongue; I may understand them better today than in the past. It's possible I may even comprehend them better than if I'd never gone to prison at all.

6:00 A.M.

Between six and seven o'clock, the five housing units of Brunswick Correctional Center are called one after another to the dining hall for breakfast. The female guard yells "Chow!", the double sliding doors in the building entryway are opened, and several dozen sleepy inmates shuffle toward the dining hall.

At this time of day during the winter months, orange-colored floodlights scan us from the top of the surrounding buildings. The color is harsh, unnatural, and ugly, causing everything to appear flat and pale, as if we were in a cheap horror movie. Even worse, the glare hides from us whatever stars may still be shining. Some of us may spend years or decades without seeing the stars, even if we hadn't long ago stopped looking to the heavens.

Brunswick is a relatively small prison, with about 700 inmates. Virginia, a state with a population of approximately seven million, has (if one includes all jails and correctional facilities) roughly 60,000 inmates.[2] This figure doesn't take into account the thousands of individuals incarcerated in military and federal prisons located in the state. In comparison, my country, Germany, with a population of 80 million, holds approximately 80,000 inmates.[3] This disparity is reflected nationwide. The U.S. has 751 prisoners for every 100,000 citizens, whereas Germany locks up only 96 out of the same number.[4] And Germany's incarceration rate is greater than the European average.[5]

The inmates from my building enter the dining hall and

stand in line. Through a small rectangular opening in the wall, almost waist-high, brown plastic trays emerge one by one, each tray exactly the same. The prisoners who work in the kitchen are completely hidden from us so that we can't signal a friend to give us a little extra to eat. That would add a couple of cents to the cost of the food.

After I've received my tray, I get coffee from a big, brown plastic container and sit at one of the many four-man metal tables. We can sit wherever we want at Brunswick, another small luxury denied us at the supermax. Like the supermax dining hall, however, everything is bolted down, even the metal stools at each table. From the guards' perspective, the dining hall is the most dangerous place in the prison, since so many inmates gather here at the same time.

Every morning, I break the fast with Harry and Richard, two veterans of the Vietnam conflict who've been serving time since the mid-1970s. The tough, browned warriors who once searched for the Viet Cong in the jungles of Southeast Asia are long gone. In their place are two overweight, slightly stooped grandfathers with age spots and a few wisps of white hair on their balding pates.

Approximately 58,000 American soldiers died during the war in Vietnam, and about the same number of veterans of that conflict still find themselves behind bars today.[6] Trained to kill and then traumatized by battle, these men returned home, committed serious crimes, and were disposed of in the correctional system. There is no therapy, much less mercy, for men like Harry and Richard. (A few veterans of the Iraq War are now trickling into prison, the first drops of a coming flood.)

Harry and Richard are my friends because we three are comrades in the constant struggle to preserve our honor and dignity in the midst of the most difficult and corrupting of circumstances. The majority of prisoners have, unfortunately, lost this struggle. They have tried to drown their misery and themselves in drugs, homemade alcohol, and "situational" homosexuality. One can understand such decisions and forgive them; but Harry, Richard, and I refuse to give in.

For us, each day is a battle in the endless war against hopelessness and inhumanity. We use our time together at breakfast to screw up our courage like soldiers have always done and will do: we trade the dirtiest jokes and the nastiest insults we can devise. Nothing is so bad that we can't laugh over it. No cruelty of the guards or of our fellow prisoners is so vile that we cannot be even crueler in our humor. Each joke and every insult are further proof to ourselves that we've not yet been crushed.

An example: In April 2004, my then cell partner committed suicide while Harry, Richard, and I were eating breakfast. The guy was asleep snoring when I left the cell for the dining hall. When I returned thirty minutes later, I found him hanging from my bunk bed—blue, stiff, and quite dead.

"It's all your fault!" said Harry as soon as he heard the news. "He must have seen your sweet behind every day and you never let him have a shot at it, you bastard!"

"'Murder by withheld affection.' Hey! That's what I'll say when I snitch to the administration," said Richard. "Think I'll get parole if I turn state's evidence?"

Harry and Richard's brutal refusal to allow me even the tiniest bit of self-pity saved me, and I'll always be indebted to them. Truly, they are my comrades in arms! And yet, aside from our suffering, I have little in common with them. Harry and Richard were frontline soldiers freshly returned from Vietnam when they landed in prison. At the time I was incarcerated, I was a recipient of an academic scholarship to the prestigious University of Virginia, the son of a German vice-consul, and an artistic soul by nature. Discussing philosophy, meditation, or medieval mysticism with these two friends would be simply impossible. Thus, I'm sometimes conscious of an internal dissonance during the rough teasing we share at breakfast. On the one hand, I really love these two vets; on the other, I recognize that we're worlds apart. The only thing that truly connects us is this wretched, miserable prison.

At times like these, I always let loose with a melodramatic groan. "I want to go hooooome!" I whine. Harry and Richard know exactly what to do. They immediately bombard me with the worst possible insults, pummeling me with their jokes. They also somehow manage to remind me that I'm not alone, that it's exactly the same for them. They want to go home, too.

This damn prison!

When we're not verbally abusing one another, Harry, Richard, and I entertain ourselves with complaints about the food—and with good reason. The U.S. spends approximately $63 billion a year to maintain its jails and penitentiaries, with Virginia alone forking out roughly one billion dollars annually.[7] Because there are about 2.3 million individuals incarcerated nationwide,[8] very little is spent on each prisoner. Virginia, for instance, allots only 61 cents per inmate meal.[9]

We receive bread and potatoes three times a day—and as little of those as possible—usually accompanied by a small quantity of meat, almost always some form of processed turkey heavily cut with soy (the cheapest meat and meat-substitute products on the market). For lunch and dinner we're also given a small portion of vegetables, with a piece of fruit at noon and some breaded concoction in the evening for dessert. The fruit should be the highlight of the three meals, but it's often bruised or nearly spoiled, because it's cheaper. Anyone who thinks I am exaggerating should try to prepare a meal for 61 cents themselves!

So what does this morning's breakfast tray look like? It contains two pancakes, both about four inches in diameter, with syrup and a lump of margarine. On the side are potatoes and oatmeal, precisely one cup's worth each—no more. Finally, we get a six-ounce bag of apple juice, which bears a suspicious resemblance to a urine sample.

We're served this kind of breakfast on two out of the five working days of the week. On the other pancake day, however, we get two small sausage links in place of the potatoes. These sausages are made from the same turkey-and-soy mixture that forms virtually all of our meat items: turkey burger, Salisbury (turkey) steak, meat (turkey) loaf, Italian (turkey) sausage, (turkey) spaghetti sauce, and many more choice recipes.

The substance is gray and tasteless, exactly like the potatoes and oatmeal. And our lives. Each meal is identical to the last, just as each day is to the one before it: insipid and boring. If just once we had orange juice instead of apple! And if only the slop they feed us had some taste to it! But no, that is just not possible.

In the Department of Corrections Head Dietician's office in Richmond, the caloric content of every inmate meal is calculated precisely so that each tray meets the minimum standard. This is why asking for a pancake tray without syrup is simply not permitted: even the syrup and margarine are included in the total calorie count and, thus, are an integral part of the meal. As each tray is prepared, the process is carefully monitored to ensure that we receive exactly what we're supposed to receive, and not the tiniest bit more.

With every meal on every tray, society reminds us how much it despises us.

7:00 A.M.

We are locked in our cells to be counted. This is the first of four daily "count times": two guards blow their whistles and look into every cell through the door window, to confirm that we're all still here. If you don't obey the order to stand when the guards reach your door, you'll get yelled at and perhaps even receive a disciplinary charge. Count time not only verifies that none of us has escaped but ensures that we obey an order at least four times each day.

My cell partner spends the quiet hour of count time dozing. We don't speak because we can't stand one another. Weeks go by without us exchanging a word, not even a "good morning." Neither he nor I have submitted a request to be moved to a different cell, even though we've each had many opportunities to do so, because almost all the other prisoners are worse. The majority of them are young blacks from urban areas, who play rap music all night long and wear their baggy prison pants so low that their underwear shows. My current cell partner and I are both white, in our early to mid-forties, and neat and quiet. With so many positives, what does it matter that we hold each other in contempt?

I use this first count time of the day to read the newspaper (lent to me by a fellow inmate), write letters, and watch twenty-minutes worth of news on my five-inch-screen television. Apart from occasional phone calls and visits, this is my only contact with the outside world. But I'm pretty well off in comparison to most other prisoners, who, instead of trying to keep abreast of political developments, watch sports, "reality TV," and music videos—almost exclusively. Even if they wanted to, they'd be unable to read a newspaper (unless, like me, they have a friend whose parents pay for a subscription) since the supply of free newspapers for each cellblock was eliminated in the mid-nineties. As a result, the majority of inmates know little more than who the President of the United States is. Even this information is of little use. What concern is politics to us when our lives aren't going to change no matter what happens in the world?

Letters and visits are scarce commodities in the penitentiary. Most family and friends forget prisoners after a few years, except perhaps for the occasional Christmas card. Visits may be even rarer. An acquaintance of mine hasn't set foot in the visiting room since the early eighties, and he's by no means an exception.

I, too, have lost all contact with my family in Germany. Fortunately, I have a large circle of friends in America who write to me often and come to visit about eight times a year. Such contact is highly unusual for someone who's served more than twenty years in prison. Really, I should be completely alone and isolated from the outside world.

The real punishment of prison is the loss of personal relationships. Once more, the irony of corrections is in operation, since this punishment not only affects the prisoner but also harms society. More than 90 percent of all inmates will be released one day—into a world they no longer know and to which they have no ties. Given this reality, the national recidivism rate of 67.5 percent is hardly surprising.[10] To put it another way: the more effectively and efficiently a penitentiary operates—that is, the more social isolation it inflicts as punishment—the worse society will suffer later.

My home country of Germany has attempted to solve the problem of disrupted personal relationships by granting occasional furloughs to its inmates. Not only is this almost unheard of in the U.S., but I also doubt it would be of much help. In prison, contact with the outside world can be a painful experience, which is why many prisoners deliberately choose to cut all ties with it. Instead of dealing with a painful reality, they escape to the fictional world of TV.

I, too, used to watch many hours of television each day, just like the majority of inmates. When you don't have your own life to live, you get one from the idiot box! But in the fall of 2000, the endless soap operas, entertainment programs about detectives, and even classical music and jazz on cassette finally became too much to bear. Every aspect of it reminded me in some way of what I'd lost.

So I stopped. Since then, I haven't listened to any music, and all I watch on TV is the news—twenty minutes in the mornings and evenings, and ten minutes at noon. Of course, even this diet still reminds me of the outside world, but news doesn't evoke as much of an emotional response as the entertainment programs do. They don't hurt as much.

At least, most of the time they don't. This morning is an exception because the breakfast news shows are doing their familiar wall-to-wall coverage of the arrest of a child murderer. The man had been recently released from prison, and on top of it all, he raped the poor child. It's always the same horrendous story.

We prisoners watch such news reports with different eyes than free persons. Because we're well aware how much honest citizens hold us in contempt, many of us are secretly a little pleased and relieved when a child murderer is pilloried on TV. Here is someone whom society despises even more than us!

The child murderer fulfills another need for us inmates in that he gives us someone *we* can hate and detest. In exactly the same way that we're looked down on, we want someone whom we can metaphorically kick and point the finger at. To believe oneself to be better than another person is an entirely human need that all of us share, whether we're incarcerated or not.

That's why child molesters, and above all child murderers, have such a hard time in the penitentiary. Because the guards don't feel obligated to protect them, these prisoners are regularly assaulted and raped by the other inmates. An acquaintance of mine was even murdered by his cell partner after it was discovered he was a child molester.[11]

When prisoners see the arrest of such a man in the news, we also experience a deep anger on top of all the other emotions. Because, unfortunately, some of these child murderers are recently released inmates, we know society's response all too well. Citizens won't ask what's being done with people in prison that would lead them to molest and murder a child shortly after their release. Instead, they'll simply demand that these people are locked up and the keys thrown away. "Don't release any inmates at all," the shout will go up, "not even one!" In this way, the child murderers on the news prevent the rest of us from achieving our freedom. At least, that's what we prisoners think.

I hear over and over again from an astonishing number of inmates a deep indignation over the manner in which the media raise a hue and cry over the victim and the victim's family. As I've indicated, the majority of all prisoners are black, and they pay close attention to these issues. They notice that the abducted and murdered children covered in the news are almost always white. They are led to two possible conclusions: either black children are never victims of such crimes, or the coverage of such crimes is a spectacle designed to boost ratings and advertising revenue. My fellow inmates logically conclude the latter and come to recognize one of the standard formulas of the infotainment industry. Once they realize the story is exactly the same each time—that only the names of the victim and the perpetrator are different—anger sets in, even though they're prisoners. They have children and families too, after all. Or at least, they had them once.

One aspect of this sensationalist reporting that outrages me in particular is that the stories lack any useful or important information. Fewer than fifty children are abducted and murdered each year in the U.S.[12] Although each of these crimes is horrible, and the suffering of the victims and the grief of their families are barely imaginable, the reality is that the average citizen has little reason to worry their son or daughter will be a victim of such a crime. Indeed, their child is more likely to be struck by lightning than abducted, raped, and murdered by a released inmate.

Instead of reassuring parents with relevant information and real facts and figures, however, news programs generate as much hysteria as possible. Every journalistic trick is used to heighten emotions, thereby obscuring the facts of the matter. And because nearly fifty children are abducted and murdered annually, the gruesome spectacle can be repeated on an almost weekly basis. This week it happens in New York, last week was California's turn, the week before, Florida. . . . Naturally, TV viewers can only conclude that their children are in the greatest danger.

No wonder public anger rises each time the police arrest another monster—me, for example. I wasn't accused of murdering a child, but I was blamed for the brutal stabbing deaths of my girlfriend's parents. But in the on-going TV series "Monster of the Week," such details are trivial and interchangeable. In the U.S., Germany, and England, my arrest was literally front-page news in the popular press. It was the lead story on the local television news, and at least an item (if not the lead) on national news broadcasts. The well-known former U.S. Senator from New York, Alphonse D'Amato, wrote an editorial about me, and preacher Jerry Fallwell gave an on-camera interview: both called for my execution. Even leading TV journalists like Larry King and Geraldo Rivera pilloried me on their programs.

All of this occurred between 1986 and 1990. Every time I watch the arrest of a high-profile murderer on television, I see . . . myself. So this morning I once again find myself forced to remember a time when *I* was public enemy number one. I know exactly what it's like to have the whole world hate you. I also comprehend every detail of what will happen to the man I'm watching on the television screen. He will, in effect, be chased into the desert.

The ritual of the scapegoat set forth in Leviticus 16:10, 20–22 hasn't changed a jot in the last three thousand years. The "Monster of the Week" show celebrates and reenacts this rite of catharsis. However, since goats and rams are no longer credible surrogates today, the "Monster of the Week" takes the animal's place. The public's hatred and anger is laid upon the "evil one" and then he or she is cast into the wasteland. The news programs are so emotionally charged and practically without fact because they aren't journalism, but a primitive religion.

My books (including this one), my daily meditation practice, and even my friendship with Harry and Richard constitute my efforts to stand before the camp of the Israelites, hammer my horns against the gate, and bleat, "Bah-ah-ah-ah-ah!" They are my statements that I'm neither the monster nor murderer nor convenient "evil one" that I've been portrayed to be.

Even though, as we shall see later, my "Monster of the Week" persona has some benefits within the prison, I nonetheless strive to remain a person with a name. I will not allow myself to be cast out into the desert.

8:00 A.M.

At eight, the cell doors are unlocked so that students can go to their classes and workers to their jobs. More importantly, my cell partner and I can take turns going to the bathroom. It may be unpalatable to hear, but in a double cell, coordinating bowel movements is a must. If my cell partner and I were to conduct our business during count time, we'd be forced to endure each other's odor and noise. One has to think about such things in prison. In extreme cases, poor scheduling of bathroom use can lead to conflicts.

After my cell partner and I have completed our dance around the toilet, it's off to work. In my case, that commute entails going through the double sliding doors of the building entryway and across to the gym. I am employed as the official toilet cleaner.

On the way to my job I pass the big-wheeled trash dumpsters that sit next to the building. Several prisoners, dressed in the green T-shirts of the yard crew, are already hanging around the area. They're pretending to ready the dumpsters for the trip to the sally port, but in fact they're waiting for the customers who live in my housing unit. As they do every morning, the green shirts distribute gambling tickets: small pieces of paper upon which are listed the games of the day in tiny, meticulous handwriting. Depending on the season, you can bet on football, basketball, baseball, and NASCAR. Many prisoners feel this is virtually their entire reason for living: the buy-in is a pack of cigarettes, and the potential payoff is fifty packs or more—worth roughly $200! As with all gambling, though, the real winner is the prisoner who runs the operation.

Many members of the yard crew work practically full-time for the betting ring, but at least occasionally they must also mow the grass, pick up cigarette butts and trash, and empty the dumpsters. If you think these aren't very desirable jobs, then I'm afraid you simply don't understand what's truly important in prison! Since the green shirts are allowed almost unrestricted movement from one end of the prison compound to the other while supposedly performing their assigned tasks, they possess something denied to almost everyone else—the tiniest scrap of freedom.

Because of this freedom, a great deal moves with the yard crew, much of it in the big rolling dumpsters. Drugs, mash, homemade knives, stolen TVs and radios, food smuggled out of the kitchen, cigarettes and tobacco to pay off the loan-sharks, and so on are carted back and forth. No guards look into the dumpsters because they know very well that they might find something that doesn't belong in there. Then the guard in question would have to write up a disciplinary charge, submit a report, and explain the incident to the shift supervisor in the watch office. . . . Given the amount of work and aggravation involved, it's much easier for the guards to look the other way and let the boys do what they want.

These boys—the yard workers with the green T-shirts—are what in penitentiary slang are called "convicts":* prisoners whose self-esteem is defined by their fundamental opposition to everything that society values. Since society has labeled

---

* This chapter explores how the terms "convict" and "inmate" are used in the penitentiary. Since prisoners define these words differently than civilians, I have put them in quotation marks throughout. In subsequent chapters, I drop the quotation marks and return to using convict and inmate as synonyms for prisoner.

them "criminals" or "offenders," they abandon themselves to this role with a passion. "Convicts" break prison rules on principle and lie to the guards consistently, even when there's no reason to. Arguments are usually resolved through violence— the more vicious the attack, the more respect one gains.

Most importantly, "convicts" enforce the "convict code," the iron rule of silence. Regardless of the subject matter, you're not allowed to provide the guards with any kind of information, or you're labeled a snitch. Such a "code" is, of course, pure madness, a value system designed by and for psychopaths. But since the prison system allows the strongest and most brutal prisoners to control and exploit the weaker ones, the code is widespread throughout the penitentiary. Even prisoners who have no desire to be "convicts" nevertheless follow the code so they can avoid being called a snitch.

In contrast to the "convicts," the "inmates" are prisoners who try to follow all the rules and comply with every order from the guards. "Inmates" also do other foolish things, like going to school to try to learn something. *Idiots!* Every "convict" knows that you only go to school to get out of work, steal something, conduct some kind of business transaction, flirt with the teacher, and so forth. To the "convicts," the "inmates" are goody-goodies who can't ever be trusted.

An outsider might think that guards would prefer to deal with "inmates" rather than "convicts." Even the "convicts" believe this, since their self-image depends so much on the idea of being the bad boys of the penitentiary. In fact, the opposite is the case.

In order to understand this seeming paradox, it's necessary to consider the guards' position. The guards are stuck in a boring job. They receive a poor salary and suffer very harsh working conditions. If, for instance, a guard sees one prisoner beating another to a pulp, why should he intervene? Both prisoners are criminals, after all, so they both deserve a good beating. Aside from that, the guard runs the risk he might himself be injured if he intervenes. And, afterwards, those damned reports have to be written. . . .

From the guard's perspective, it's obviously much smarter simply to allow the prisoners to resolve their problems among themselves. For that to work, one requires reliable and sensible assistants to ensure that the violence doesn't get out of hand and no one snitches to the administration. What every savvy guard really needs, therefore, is . . . a well-organized group of "convicts." With this group in place, everyone's problems are solved: the guards can nap at their posts, the "convicts" can exploit their fellow prisoners, and the supervisors in the watch office are kept blissfully ignorant. The only ones who could possibly disrupt this perfect little world are those damned "inmates," with their so-called principles.

Once again, we come across the irony of corrections. Instead of the guards educating prisoners on how to become better human beings, the "convicts" gently and quietly seduce the guards into following the convict code. Unfortunately, the irony of corrections extends even further in this case: in the existential circumstance of life behind bars, the "inmate" way of thinking isn't necessarily better than the "convict" mentality. The former can end up even more corrupted and ruined than the latter.

Every prisoner is held against his will for the intentional infliction of pain: this is the meaning of punishment. If a private citizen were to act in such a way toward another it would be considered abduction and torture. Society may consider such treatment toward prisoners justified, but in the eyes of prisoners, pain is pain, regardless of the legal validation behind it.

What the "inmates" do—and what for them is so psychologically dangerous—is to turn to their abductors and torturers and ask for help. Abused children and women in similar situations often do the same; psychologists call this defense mechanism the Stockholm Syndrome, which is when the victim identifies with the abuser. In prison, the syndrome can lead many "inmates" to act as though they were deputy guards.

For example, some "inmates" spend the entire day composing written complaints about obscure rule violations: "Yesterday I saw inmate so-and-so light a cigarette in a non-smoking area and the guard didn't say anything to him!" Other "inmates" develop slave-like submissiveness, especially toward correctional staff in higher positions, often with strong feelings of friendship and love that sometimes reach the level of fantasy. The worst, however, are the confidential informants who act as spies for the administration. As in the outside world, most informants are instigators, since they need a constant stream of investigative successes to ensure their favored position.

Not every "inmate" becomes a Judas, although the tendency points in that direction. Neither does every "convict" become a prison mafioso—some may even mutate into garden gangsters! This is what happened with Sylvester, a rail-thin black man in his mid-fifties who's never without a lit cigarette and leads the green-shirted yard crew.

Sylvester has nothing to do with the gambling operation, outside of placing an occasional bet or two. In the past, he'd undoubtedly been involved in business dealings typical to the "convict"—he'd been doing time since 1981, after all. However, over the years and decades, a man becomes older, wiser, and sometimes milder. Nowadays, Sylvester leaves the betting ring, the pornography trade, the drug trafficking, and other businesses of that sort to the younger prisoners.

Instead, Sylvester focuses on his official job, one of the most important in the prison. Brunswick Correctional Center is a relatively old facility, and therefore has many grassy areas that must be mowed and maintained. Sylvester does a superb job of organizing it all. The boys of the yard crew obey him because he's one of them, and the guards permit only him to use the huge riding lawnmower. Several years ago a warden said, "If Sylvester wants me to personally hand him the very first tray in the dining hall every day, then that's what I'll do."

Sylvester, however, is not an "inmate" but a "convict," which means he doesn't break his back for the sake of the damn prison, but to put money in his own pocket. As a result, he's always working some angle or circumventing some rule. Sylvester's unofficial vegetable gardens can be found all over Brunswick Correctional Center: behind the parking area of the kitchen warehouse, next to the segregation unit, in the fenced-in spot at the rear of the infirmary where the nurses go to smoke, and so on. Sylvester knows every corner of the compound and all the best plots of land—the many, little half-forgotten places where hardly anyone looks. Here he's planted cucumbers, tomatoes, watermelon, and many other vegetables and plants that to us prisoners are pure, divine, priceless luxuries.

With these fruits and vegetables, Sylvester buys the cooperation of staff members who are posted near his gardens. "Cooperation" means that the nurses "fail" to notice that a small vegetable plot has suddenly cropped up behind the infirmary and, paradoxically, everyone knows that these plants are under the protection of the medical staff, so no one dares touch them. At harvest time, the most beautiful watermelons in the world magically appear in the infirmary.

None of this is legal. If you had a mind to, you could even consider the vegetable gardens to be a violation of the rules, and the watermelon a form of attempted bribery. An "inmate" would certainly see it that way. But, luckily for all of us, the prison administrators follow the convict code and stroll right past Sylvester's gardens with a blind eye. No doubt, they too

occasionally receive a few sun-ripened, freshly picked tomatoes wrapped in newspaper.

"Convicts" call this "paying taxes."

This morning, as I pass by Sylvester and his yard crew on
my way to work, I can't help but think back to the days when
I myself received my tiny share of "taxes." A few years ago, I
had a fairly important, influential prison job (more on that in
a later chapter), so a few cucumbers came my way from time
to time. They were wonderful.

Nowadays, however, I clean toilets in the gym. Sylvester
always has a friendly greeting for me, but I haven't seen a
single cucumber in years.

On the way from the housing unit to my place of work I pass between the watch office on my right and the infirmary on my left. I turn right through the gate in the fence that encircles the recreation yard, and right again through the rear door of the gymnasium. Situated approximately in the center of the five housing units, the gym is also the center of penitentiary life. It's where we prisoners work off our frustration and stress by playing basketball and lifting weights instead of fighting and raping each other.

Since Brunswick Correctional Center is a model prison, more sports and recreational activities are available to us here than in other prisons. This feature is essentially an attempt to control us with a lighter hand. Astonishingly, it actually works.

It isn't necessary to blast people with rubber pellets, as happened to me at the supermax, to have power over them. Just as effective is the mere threat to cancel the upcoming basketball tournament. In both cases, the guards are exercising control over us, compelling us to obey and denying our freedom. The "land of liberty" busily perfects the use of both carrots and sticks.

The almighty dollar is used to keep us leashed as well. In addition to reducing meal costs to 61 cents, the correctional system limits other daily necessities to the absolute mini-mum—or less. It is next to impossible to acquire an extra roll of toilet paper, for instance. Anyone who wants to wipe his butt properly must have a job to buy additional toilet paper from the prison store. From this perspective, the $22 to $54 the prison administration pays us each month for our work is a highly economical and efficient means of control.

Even more important than our wages, though, are the little extras on the side that come with many jobs. Sylvester's vegetable garden is entirely typical in this regard. Workers in the prison laundry give out brand new underwear in exchange for a pack of cigarettes. Kitchen workers regularly smuggle food to their customers in the housing units. Maintenance department workers unofficially repair or modify TVs, radios, and fans. And the list goes on. Who's going to work 120 hours a month for the laughable sum of $22?

Guards not only tolerate prisoners earning a little on the side, they even encourage it. They can reward inmates by turning a blind eye to theft, and by allowing prisoners to steal, the guards also gain power over them. (Theft is illegal, after all!) Consequently, inmates will occasionally ply the guards with packs of cigarettes, to counter the implicit threat of a disciplinary charge. These are the same "taxes" that Sylvester the garden gangster pays. Once the guards have been compromised in this way, they can hardly report a theft to the watch office. In this manner, the actual work of the prison becomes little more than camouflage that obscures the systematic looting of anything small and portable enough to be sold or bartered.

Once again, we find ourselves confronted with the irony of corrections. On the one hand, inmates wouldn't work at all if they weren't allowed to steal or gain other advantages through their jobs. On the other, prisoners become trained to regard every job only as an opportunity for theft and graft. It's the same for the guards. They, too, look for ways to improve their income by smuggling in pornography, drugs, and other illicit items. What's good enough for the inmate goose is certainly good enough for the guard gander.

Except in my case. The gymnasium toilets don't have any high-value items to steal. My job as the toilet cleaner is just about the most undesirable and degrading work assignment in the entire penitentiary. No other prisoner is willing to perform this task because the gym bathroom is normally one of the busiest bordellos at Brunswick. I have to clean up not only feces and urine, but also blood and sperm.

The blood and sperm are another feature of the prison economy. Because there are more inmates than jobs, prisoners without employment must find another way to earn money. So some resort to prostitution. And someone must clean up afterward. I am that anonymous someone: the janitor for the penitentiary whorehouse.

To be honest, recently my job hasn't been as disgusting as it was in the past. Several months ago, the correctional sex trade was forced to relocate because the gym bathroom came under closer scrutiny. A guard posted in the gym foolishly allowed himself to be caught in the act of smuggling in steroids and pornography. The subsequent investigation revealed that the gym bathroom was being used as a bordello, so the enterprise had to be moved elsewhere—outsourced, as it were. Fortunately for me, the prostitutes, and their customers, the Porta-John™ in the recreation yard became the new, somewhat cramped assignation spot.

As well as decontaminating the toilet for the inmates, I also clean the bathroom used by the guards who supervise the gym. Since I'm somewhat reliable and competent, the guards consider me a good worker. Once, one of the new guards even uttered the word "thanks" to me after I finished cleaning the toilet. I was so surprised that I was actually speechless for a few seconds. So touched was I by this expression of gratitude that I took the time to explain to the new guard that he'd committed a terrible faux pas: human beings do not thank subhumans! As a reward for this sage advice, he allowed me to steal a roll of toilet paper.

Once again, all was right in our little world.

After cleaning the toilets I get some exercise. I ran my usual seven miles yesterday, so today it's time to lift some weights. As with every other activity in the penitentiary, weightlifting is almost completely racially segregated. The whites sweat and grunt in one corner while the blacks do the same in the other. In the morning, the little weight-room radio pumps out rap music; in the afternoon, it's heavy metal. Open conflict over the weights is rare, however, since no one wants to lose this privilege.

In the weight room, of all places, the hope and despair of the prisoner's soul are revealed for all to see. These men, like all of us, possess the urge to improve themselves. How they labor and strive to train every single little muscle perfectly! If only this intense focus and energy were invested in education, with brain cells being trained as well as muscles! But this idea has never occurred to those men, and no one has taken the time to convey this thought. How will they ever rise out of their current condition?

For me, the urge to lift weights sprang from an altogether different psychological origin than that of self-improvement. I took up pumping iron in response to the sheer terror I experienced after I was very nearly raped.

It happened in the winter of 1991–92, and it occurred just as in a bad prison movie. As I stepped out of the shower, a huge black weightlifter threw me up against the tier railing, pressed his stiff penis into the small of my back, and grunted

35

into my ear, "Wha' choo gonna do if I drag you in my cell right now?" I still remember clearly how the female guard on the tier below deliberately lowered her eyes to her tabloid newspaper and turned the page. I shrieked something—I can't recall exactly what—and, astonishingly, the guy let me go.

When I think back on this event today, I'm amazed at how lucky I was. Repeated anonymous surveys have determined that 20 percent of all inmates are forced to have sex each year, and 10 percent are violently raped.[13] The overwhelming majority of these crimes are never reported: a silence maintained out of fear of retaliation from the perpetrators and because of the indifference of prison officials. In 2004, only 8,210 sexual assaults were documented,[14] even though correctional experts testifying at a U.S. Senate hearing in 2003 estimated the actual number of cases to range from 250,000 to 600,000 *per year*.[15]

By all rights, I should have been one of those victims. Instead, I escaped and ran stark naked down the tier to my cell and did my best to calm down. *What the hell was I going to do now?* I thought to myself. Snitching was out of the question: my would-be rapist had many friends who'd avenge him for such a transgression of the convict code. *Well, how about obtaining a shank—a homemade knife—and lying in wait for my assailant?* Although this would certainly earn me a great deal of respect from the other convicts, I wasn't sure I could follow through with it. Still, I had to do something! So I threw myself into weightlifting and running. And with whom did I end up pumping iron for some two years? With Joe, of course—my would-be rapist.

At the prison where this took place, the weights were located in the recreation yard. It happened to be wintertime, and we were the only idiots willing to brave the snow and ice in order to work out on that cold morning when we ran into each other. Since the guards preferred to remain in the warm indoors, the two of us were by ourselves.

Joe must have asked himself, *Should I go after this white boy again?* I certainly asked myself, *Should I take this forty-pound dumbbell and smash his skull while he's doing his bench press?* For some reason, we both decided not to act. It turns out some things are more important than sex or vengeance. Like lifting weights.

Joe died of AIDS some years ago, and so nowadays, I pump iron by myself. I choose to exercise alone because many prisoners use weightlifting as an excuse to show off and play the "big man." Such things often lead to conflict, which I prefer to avoid whenever possible. Plus, it's not at all a bad survival strategy to keep to yourself, and to be a bit different or enigmatic (but not *too* different or enigmatic!) to the other inmates. What has helped me especially in this regard is not so much that I've lifted weights alone and have always maintained my distance from others, but the "Monster of the Week" syndrome. The gruesome details of the double murder for which I was convicted were common knowledge, and that's afforded me a certain amount of protection.

I once had desperate need of this protection, since violence is an inescapable part of daily life in the correctional system. There's not much I haven't seen in the many years of incarceration.[16] Once, I was standing next to a sex offender when someone threw boiling hot water on him. Another time, I witnessed two prisoners raping a third. Back when I was still playing cards, an inmate at a neighboring table was bludgeoned from behind with a metal cigarette-butt can, his blood splattering all the way over to our table. It's probably pure coincidence that I haven't seen a murder.

The particulars of these events are of minor importance. It's not so much the violence itself that grinds you down but the sense of being in constant peril. You have to watch your back whenever you walk down the housing-unit staircase. You never know when three convicts might suddenly leap past you to pounce on the man directly in front of you and commence beating him to a bloody pulp. You can only be thankful that this time it didn't happen to you, and then walk past the melee as if you didn't see anything at all. This is the convict code.

In each of the conflicts described above, the cause was always trivial. One man, whom I befriended during the 1990s, several years earlier murdered a fellow inmate over a single pack of cigarettes. The last stabbing that tangentially involved me was triggered by a basketball game. Since you never know what might offend some idiot, you have to be on guard constantly and always expect the unexpected. As a result, as time goes by you isolate yourself more and more from other people.

Fortunately, Brunswick Correctional Center sees far fewer assaults and rapes than other facilities. But violence is only one of many reasons why you become a recluse in the penitentiary. Since so many prisoners are destitute, you always have to be on the lookout against thievery and scams. I was once even cheated out of two hardboiled eggs and a stamp. You want to have some compassion for men who are *that* desperate. But in prison other inmates are always observing you, and you simply can't afford to display any signs of weakness. If you do, the sharks begin to circle.

What is even more corrosive of your faith in other human beings are people who prove to be false friends. At the beginning of the 1990s, I befriended a guy for about two years. I thought we had a good understanding of one another, something extremely valuable in such a lonely life. He was someone who had my back, my "stickman" in prison parlance—someone who'd stick with me through thick and thin. But one day he just stopped speaking to me. When I confronted him about it, he said he was tired of waiting for me to have sex with him. Somehow, he'd gotten the impression that my homophobia was a façade.

I felt horribly betrayed. After my near-rape, I'd sought out one person with whom I could form a genuine friendship, and I thought I'd found one with this man. He'd even confided to me that several years before he'd been raped by some other prisoners. Looking back, I can understand how my ersatz stickman probably felt as betrayed as I did. He'd followed the rules of penitentiary life—for a full two years!—and then I'd cheated him out of his prize.

After a period of time, I took heart and dared to enter into yet another ordinary, non-sexual friendship. Immediately, I found myself in the same situation all over again.

And again. And again. And again. And again. And again.

In all, I have found my friendships compromised seven times—at least that's the number I can recall. You have to suppress so much in order to survive in here.

Harry and Richard, my breakfast-club companions, probably aren't faking their friendship just to get into my pants. But Harry's case is a perfect illustration of yet one more reason why inmates increasingly isolate themselves after so many years. We simply cannot offer genuine comfort to one another in these cruel circumstances.

A while back, Harry told me about his wife. He'd gotten married in 1991, after being locked up for about a decade and a half. Every weekend she came to visit him, and each year she nervously waited with him for the answer to his request for parole. Every year his application was denied because of the serious nature of his crime. Harry's wife put up with this for another decade and a half, and then turned in her divorce papers. Now Harry doesn't have a home to be released to, even if he could make parole.

That's what he told me. What can I say to him? I've heard the same sad story from at least a dozen other prisoners. I have no hope to offer him, no way to tell him that somehow things will get better. In fact, they'll only get worse. The next ten to twenty years will be even lonelier for him, and then he'll croak in some prison hospital. Alone. Anything else I could say to him would be nonsense and lies.

Harry and I both know this, so it's better if we don't talk with one another about our lives. Sometimes, though, in the early morning peace of the dayroom, we sit together in silence. Perhaps this is better than nothing at all. Perhaps not.

10:00 A.M.

At ten we have a "gate break," a ten-minute period during which the sliding double doors of the housing units are opened and the gates to the recreation yard, etc., are unlocked, so we can move from one part of the compound to another. I leave the gym sweaty from my workout and cross the rec yard to the prison store.

Because Brunswick Correctional Center was built in 1981, its recreation yard is relatively large, with a softball field, horseshoe pits, basketball, handball, and even tennis courts. Three times a week, on those days that I run instead of lifting weights, I circle the softball field on a gravel jogging-track. Now and then I allow myself to consider how nice it would be to make my runs in a straight line. Boy, what a feeling that must be. . . .

An electrified and razor-wire fence three layers deep encloses three sides of the rec yard. Since it's chain link fencing, we can clearly see the parking lot on the other side: one of the guards has a Harley Davidson! We can also see a copse, a pond with geese, cows grazing on a pasture, and the neighboring prisons. It's truly a luxury for us to be able to view all of this. Newer correctional centers, such as the supermax Wallens Ridge, have been built so that the housing units encircle a small, closed yard, in order to prevent any sight of the outside world.

One of the two neighboring facilities is Brunswick Work Center, a small minimum-security unit for females. Occasionally, we can watch the women through the fence while they work in the fields, but it's a sad spectacle. For us, women represent freedom, but these female inmates wear the same prison uniform we do.

The other facility within sight of our rec yard is Lawrenceville Correctional Center, a modern private prison. About 114,000 inmates rot in these corporate-owned penitentiaries—an enormous industry whose profits depend on feeding prisoners even less food, cutting back even further on toilet paper, and paying guards even lower wages than their counterparts in state-run facilities.[17] Squeezing costs at any cost leads to huge problems, of course, as Lawrenceville Correctional Center is currently demonstrating to the world.

As I write this, our neighbor is under investigation by the FBI. Two guards have already been convicted of drug smuggling, and it's a good bet that soon the feds will bust the prostitution ring of female guards who earn extra income from wealthy inmates. To top it all off, a lieutenant is currently under indictment for extorting $2,000 in protection money from a prisoner.[18] Such is the brave new world of the private correctional industry!

As I enter Brunswick's prison store—a small building bordering the rec yard—I encounter another manifestation of this business model. The "store" consists of a short, narrow hallway with three barred windows on one side. Stopping at the second window, I push my prison ID card through the hatch at the bottom, and the items that I ordered yesterday are quickly passed to me. In the penitentiary you have to wait for absolutely everything—except in the prison store. When it comes to getting our money, staff members suddenly become paragons of entrepreneurial efficiency and speed. But at what price?

For twenty years, state employees operated the store, and the profits were used for the benefit of the inmates. With the so-called "commissary fund," the prison administration bought softball bats and gloves, as well as weights and basket-balls for the gym. At Christmastime, each of the 700 inmates received a gift bag of chocolate, candy, and extra socks—the only Christmas presents many of us ever saw.

But in 2002, all prison stores in Virginia were leased to the Keefe Corporation. The employees who'd previously operated the store had to retrain to become guards or accept a pay reduction and toil for Keefe. Prices immediately and drastically increased, especially on toiletries and other necessities. A pack of aspirin now costs five times what it did before, even though it's exactly the same brand and packaging. Rather than using income from the prison store to benefit the inmates, profits now go to Keefe's headquarters in far-away Missouri. Now the taxpayer pays for the softball bats and basketballs, and the gift bag at Christmastime has gone.

(In July 2006, the director of the Florida Department of Corrections, James Crosby, was convicted of accepting a $130,000 bribe from a subsidiary of Keefe.[19] I couldn't possibly believe that something like that would never happen in Virginia.)

Even without such obvious corruption, prisoners are exploited mercilessly at every opportunity. On weekends, we receive only two fabulous 61-cent meals. In the visiting room, the order forms of the American Commissary Supply Company are prominently displayed, so that hungry inmates can point to them as they beg their families for additional food. For a single in-state phone call that would otherwise cost $3.00, MCI WorldCom demands $8.40, only because the telephone is located behind penitentiary walls.[20] In place of the famously indestructible prison boots of yore, today prisoners receive only dirt-cheap, flimsy plastic slip-ons, so that we're forced to buy a real tennis shoe from Keefe.

Most exploitative of all, Keefe has an exclusive contract with Virginia that permits them to charge us the full price of the tennis shoes. Keefe operates a subsidiary named Access that sells the same tennis shoes at a 40 percent discount through mail order to prisoners in states without exclusive contracts. The same principle applies to radios, TVs, and clothing as well. We always pay 40 percent more, because we *have* to buy from Keefe.

The financial exploitation of inmates is conversation topic number two in the penitentiary, immediately behind football and basketball scores. Every other week, it seems, the system finds a new way to exploit us. Recently, nurses were forbidden to provide us with small tubes of skin cream without charge, because Keefe complained that not enough cream was being sold in their store. Each one of these episodes infuriates us, because we already have too little money. The skin cream, which we now must buy from Keefe, costs us the equivalent of a full day's pay.

The Keefe way of doing business has not only a practical but also an educational effect. On the way back from the prison store to the housing unit, I have a conversation with a black kid who illustrates this point with disturbing perfection. He sees in Keefe a model of how to conduct his own life. As a table cleaner in the dining hall, he earns about $22 a month, the minimum wage. His entire month's pay is in his hands: four plastic bags of rolling tobacco, three of which he owes to a loan shark.

So how does he get his soap, toothpaste, and deodorant? "I'll get it from the rough," he says. If Keefe has the right to exploit him, why shouldn't he do the same thing to someone else? That question is not as simple to answer as you might think, given the exigencies of our situation. What are his alternatives? Prostituting himself in the gym bathroom so he can get a bottle of shampoo?

More probably, the young table cleaner will seek out an elderly white prisoner and either extort money or steal from him: "get it from the rough." He will turn the older white man into his milch cow in exactly the same way as the correctional capitalists Keefe and MCI WorldCom have turned this youth into theirs. When this kid is released, he'll skillfully employ the Keefe method in the outside world. Another irony of corrections!

Even though the next gate break isn't until eleven, the table cleaner and I are allowed through the recreation yard gate so we can return to our respective housing units. The guard is able to see that we're carrying our purchases from the prison store, and Keefe is more important than the sacred gate break schedule! As Keefe's young disciple turns right toward his building, I turn left in the direction of the "honor building." It's supposed to be an honor to live here, or rather a reward for good behavior.

Because it isn't gate break at the moment, the double sliding doors at the building entryway are closed. The female guard knows me, however, and she opens the doors with the push of a button and waves me through. In the small hallway I pass by the MCI WorldCom telephone and contemplate with pleasure the fact that Bernie Ebbers, the former CEO of that company, is now himself serving time behind bars for fraud.[21] Hopefully, he has to pay those absurd MCI prison rates too, just like us.

Even when there's no one to call, the MCI telephone can be surprisingly useful. Every once in a while an inmate becomes infatuated with the female guard posted in the housing unit control room, and although he doesn't have anyone to call, he'll position himself at the phone to watch the guard as she presses her little buttons. How romantic!

Sometimes the jailhouse Romeo will go so far as to slide his hand down his pants and begin to pleasure himself, an act that can lead to a short vacation in the segregation unit's isolation cells—or perhaps not. In fact, a secret brotherhood of inmates keeps a list of every female guard who finds it a compliment to have prisoners openly masturbate in front of them. I'm told the list is not short.

I step through the door of the dayroom and carry my Keefe purchases past a small group of card players. One of them looks up and calls out, "Hey, I see you've given Keefe a few more dollars so I can stay here longer."

"That's because I'm completely rehabilitated," I shoot back. "I've finally recognized that we both deserve much, much more punishment, and I'm even ready to pay for it with my own money."

All of the card players laugh out loud at hearing the term "rehabilitated." Every one of them has gone for years or decades without committing any rule violations, which is why we're housed in the honor building. Even the prison administrators quite publicly acknowledge that we're trustworthy.

The honor building often has only a single female guard to watch over approximately ninety inmates living on two floors (when she's not in the control room gabbing with her colleague, that is). Everyone knows that we don't need to be guarded. Except during the five daily count times, our cell-doors remain unlocked from four in the morning until well after midnight. There's probably less crime where we live than in *your* neighborhood.

But the pleasant appearance of our situation is deceiving. In the other housing units, the honor building is sometimes called "death row." Many residents will never leave prison, except in a body bag. Either they are incarcerated for life, or their sentences are so long that it hardly makes any difference. The majority of my fellow residents have, like me, already served more than twenty years behind bars. Many have even done more than thirty. Neither the time served nor our excellent behavior reports interest the parole board in the least.

As a result, the atmosphere of the honor building is virtually tomb-like. In the dayroom you see only old men with gray hair and fat bellies sitting around and complaining about their arthritis and high blood pressure. Why should they even bother getting up in the morning? Every few months we have yet another memorial service for one of our "dinosaurs" who's made "horizontal parole."

Many of the inmates I describe in this book live in the honor building: my breakfast club buddies Harry and Richard, for example, and Sylvester the garden gangster. But not all prisoners deal with the losses we inevitably experience as well as these three. Eugene is a nightmare of a convict. He's permanently nasty, his teeth are stained with tobacco, and he has a potbelly and unshaven jowls. This morning he isn't playing cards with the others in the dayroom but is instead sitting in the room around the corner with the washer and dryer, smoking a hand-rolled cigarette.

Eugene was thirty-two years old when he committed a murder in 1984. Because he'd never been in trouble with the law before, he dutifully reported his crime to the police and pled guilty in court. His honesty impressed no one: he received a life sentence with an additional two years for the use of a firearm.

In 1997, Eugene became eligible to apply for parole for the first time. He allowed himself to hope that he just might make it, since he'd received not a single disciplinary charge during his entire time in prison. Nevertheless, the parole board said no. Eugene had his first heart attack, followed by a four-way bypass operation. Since then, Eugene has been on a daily regimen of seven different medications and is allowed only light-duty work—sweeping the dayroom floor and wiping tables, earning the prison's minimum wage. He supplements his income by washing the clothes of other inmates who work all day.

Recently, Eugene began to experience excruciating pain in his right leg, requiring yet another trip to the hospital. The doctors told him the pain in his leg has nothing to do with his heart condition or poor circulation, but Eugene has his doubts. Now he must wait for further testing . . . and wait and wait and wait some more, since these tests are very expensive.

In 2001, after he'd received his third "turn-down" for parole, Eugene's family wrote him a letter to notify him formally that they'd now finally given up hope of him ever being released, and that they were therefore severing all ties with him. Since that time, he's received only a postcard from his brother. Eugene submitted one more application for parole and then gave up himself: in 2006 he didn't even attend his interview with the representative of the parole board. No one—neither a guard, caseworker, or administrator—asked him why. Everyone knows that Eugene is going to die in prison.

Eugene's only pride and joy is the tattoo he had etched into his chest after his heart attack, directly over the fresh scar from the bypass operation. The tattoo depicts a naked woman hanging upside down from a giant meat hook pierced through her genitals. He displays this ghastly image with great pleasure, reveling in the shocked expressions on the faces of the most hardened convicts.

In the dining hall, Eugene also delights in describing what he'd like to do to the facility's Food Service Director whenever she dishes up some particularly nauseating slop. I won't give you the details of his revenge fantasies, but German shepherds often play a role. As with the tattoo, Eugene's goal is to disgust and revolt others with his comments and cause us to wonder what kind of monster could invent such things, much less say them out loud.

Eugene isn't a monster, nor is he especially crazy. He is simply without hope and full of despair, and he wants someone to notice, perhaps even to care. Since no one is concerned in the least with his suffering, Eugene must instead be satisfied with the revulsion he deliberately provokes in others.

He and I talk about these things on occasion—I don't believe he discusses them with any of the other prisoners— and sometimes it all just pours out of him: the world hates him, he hates the world, and the only thing he looks forward to now is death. To hasten that blessed release, Eugene eats as many fatty foods and smokes as many unfiltered cigarettes as he possibly can. He's hoping for another heart attack, and soon, and wishes it might be the last one.

As I interviewed Eugene for this chapter, I asked him whether in some sense the tattoo on his chest represents himself. I was somewhat nervous as I questioned him about this, since Eugene is a fairly large man and subject to extreme mood swings (which is why he must take antidepressants on a daily basis).

Eugene, however, immediately understood what I was getting at, and he confirmed my suspicion. The parole board that won't let him go, his family that abandoned him after nineteen years, the world that has rejected him—they've done to him exactly what you see depicted on his chest. That's what his life feels like, as if *he* had been pierced through the genitals and hung upside down to rot. Every second for him is pure agony.

For many residents of the honor building, Eugene is a kind of cautionary example, since we're almost in the same situation as he. If we're not yet there already, it won't be too much longer before we too become old, sick, alone, and destitute. Eugene perhaps comprehends the reality of our condition more clearly than any of us are able or willing to. In a way, all of us are Eugene.

Because 27.5 percent of all inmates are sentenced to more than twenty years, American penitentiaries will house more and more Eugenes.[22] Only 8.6 percent of the current U.S.

prison population is classified as "elderly," but this percentage is projected to increase to 25 percent by the year 2025.[23] The Bureau of Justice Statistics has calculated that only 2 percent of all elderly prisoners would recidivate if they were to be released.[24] But that's an unlikely "if."

What makes this situation so insane is the fact that it costs three times as much to keep an old and sickly inmate behind bars as it does a young healthy man—about $69,000 per year.[25] Those who think this is a colossal waste of money still don't have a grasp of the new business model of American corrections. For companies that specialize in supplying state and private correctional facilities with medical services, that $69,000 is pure potential profit.

At Brunswick Correctional Center, the infirmary is operated by Prison Health Services, a firm known for allowing more than two-dozen prisoners to die under pitiful circumstances in New York and Florida.[26] Nevertheless, the company remains a popular partner for correctional managers across the nation because it assumes full legal liability for medically related issues. In return, Prison Health Services is allowed to cut costs to the bone. So long as profits continue to rise, what does it matter if a few offenders die?

The older inmates housed with me in the honor building are the perfect raw material for this business model. Since most elderly prisoners have already lost all contact with the outside world, they present a much lower risk that outraged family members will sue the company when yet another incarcerated patient dies. It's only logical that private companies are often contracted to operate the new geriatric prisons being built all over the country to accommodate the growing number of elderly prisoners. The old and helpless are the most profitable inmates of all.

As I arrive at my cell, I'm not thinking about the financial advantages of elderly prisoners. I set my grocery bag on the collapsible table (locking away my purchases in the metal locker isn't necessary in the honor building) and strip down to my underwear. It's off to the shower to wash off the sweat from my workout. Being able to shower anytime is a true luxury: in some prisons, you're allowed to shower only three or four times a week.

The showers in the honor building have an additional advantage in that the curtains don't have any holes in them. In the other housing units, almost all of the shower curtains are riddled with peepholes at eye level so that the "young bucks" can watch the female guards in the dayroom while they masturbate. This isn't a problem in the honor building, thank goodness: at our age, we're all nearsighted or impotent.

After I've dried myself off and put on a clean set of clothes, I return to the dayroom. My cell partner is returning from work, and he should have a few minutes to himself in the cell before we're locked in again for the next count time. Since our daily routine never varies, we don't need to discuss this with one another. And that's good, because we really can't stand each other.

In the dayroom I run into Mrs. Jefferson, who, as usual, yells, "Stop it, Soering, stop it!"

"Stop what, Mrs. Jefferson?" I dutifully ask, as I do every time.

"Being so sexy—stop it, Soering, just stop it!" she calls, slapping her hands on her thighs and cackling so loud that the card players turn around to look.

Mrs. Jefferson is my favorite guard, a black grandmother in her late fifties from Chicago. She was a guard there, too—"in a real prison, not like here," she always declares proudly—and then a few years ago, she moved to the warmer climate of Virginia to enjoy an early retirement. But that was too boring: like many released inmates, she missed the familiar world of prison.

"Soering, my daughter called me from Chicago," she tells me now. "'Mama,' she said, 'Mama, I think I'm going to become a lesbian.'"

"Why's that?" I ask.

"Because all the black men are behind bars! There's no black men left, Soering—they've all gone away."

And with that, Mrs. Jefferson has gotten on to her favorite

subject: racism in the correctional system. Even though only 12 percent of the U.S. population is African-American, 68 percent of all prisoners in America are either black or Hispanic.[27] One out of three black men will spend some portion of his life behind bars.[28] In many metropolitan areas, like Mrs. Jefferson's Chicago, more than 50 percent of young black men are incarcerated, on parole or probation, or out on bail.[29] These statistics demonstrate why approximately half of the security staff at Brunswick Correctional Center are African-American women like Mrs. Jefferson. Because so many black men have prior felony convictions, they're barred from working in corrections.

Mrs. Jefferson knows all about these issues, since she's both a child of the big city and a northerner. "These blacks here in the South still have slavery in their heads," she often remarks. "I can't believe what they let whites do to them! But I'm a Yankee, so I buck—that's why I've never been promoted!"

Because I'm German, Mrs. Jefferson does not consider me white. I have no part in the complicated history of slavery and racism in America, so I don't bear any part of the collective white guilt. Not only that, but in her opinion my German citizenship also makes me an expert in an area that fascinates her: genocide. Mrs. Jefferson wants to talk about that today, too.

"Soering, Soering, I have something new out of the *Washington Post*," she says. "A big study by the University of California. From 1982 till 1996, several researchers followed a group of 850,000 blacks."

"And what were their findings?"

"In 1982 this group had exactly the same number of AIDS cases as an equivalent white population. But in 1996 there were seven times as many. Seven times! Guess why."

"Because more blacks are sent to prison than whites, and AIDS is rampant in here?"[30]

"Exactly! See, you Germans get it—you've had experience

with that sort of thing. This is genocide, mass murder, a Holo-
caust!"

I once tried to explain to Mrs. Jefferson that such remarks
were considered taboo in Germany, due to the historical
uniqueness of the Nazi crimes. She reacted sharply: "It's pure
racism," she said, to consider the life of a white Jew to be more
important than the life of a black American. She gave me a
look that let me know she was wondering if I wasn't a little bit
white after all.

What I really would've liked to have said to Mrs. Jefferson
was that she was actually whiter than I am. The truth of the
matter is that *she* is the one who earns her living in the enormous business-machine of American corrections—the modern
form of slavery. Approximately 750,000 guards, managers,
nurses, doctors, teachers, and caseworkers are employed in this
nation's 4,573 jails and prisons, and their recession-proof jobs
are just as important to these people as profits are to Keefe,
MCI WorldCom, and Prison Health Services.[31] The last thing
Mrs. Jefferson can afford is prison reform and less slavery!

The California Correctional Peace Officers Association
(CCPOA) even advocates for more prisons by giving millions
of dollars in campaign donations to politicians who demand
longer prison sentences.[32] Virginia is little different. When
then-governor Mark Warner attempted to shut down three
small, outdated prisons in 2002, there were public hearings, a
petition with six thousand signatures, and even a demonstra-
tion in the state capitol of Richmond. Brunswick Correctional
Center was one of the three facilities slated to be closed—to
the great consternation of Mrs. Jefferson.[33]

What finally decided the issue was most likely the intervention of state senator Louise L. Lucas. Two of the three
endangered correctional centers are located in her district,
called Southside. Mrs. Lucas, an African-American herself,
was known to speak out occasionally on behalf of the (mostly

black) inmates and their families—one of the very few politicians to do so.

So what kind of appeal did the black senator make to the white governor? "Hopefully your conscience will say to you, 'We can't do this to Southside.'"[34] Southside has no other industry besides prisons. The jobs of the (mostly black) guards were simply more important than the freedom of the (mostly black) prisoners. If the guards lost their jobs, then Mrs. Lucas might lose hers at the next election. Consequently, the governor only closed one small prison in a predominantly white district in northern Virginia and left alone "her" two correctional facilities. Mrs. Jefferson had it right: here, in the South, folks still have slavery in their heads.

Such a mindset applies to inmates, too. It's an unfortunate fact of life that systematic, lifelong discrimination doesn't ennoble the people victimized by that discrimination. Instead, it embitters them. When a victim then gets the opportunity to exact revenge, he often does so without mercy. This is especially true in America's penitentiaries. Because blacks finally find themselves in the majority, prison society is a kind of distorted mirror image of civil society. The predominantly black guards play along: at every opportunity, from food service jobs to passing out toilet paper, black prisoners receive preferential treatment.

Even with sex, race plays a huge role. Blacks can have either white or black "punks" as "wives," and whites can subjugate other whites. But no white is ever allowed to have a black "punk." It's simply not done!

As far as I know, only Human Rights Watch has had the courage to speak openly about this issue, principally in their report *No Escape: Male Rape in U.S. Prisons.*[35] Why is almost everyone else unwilling to talk about this topic? It may be because sex and racism may be the only remaining taboos in America, and because many whites still feel so much of that collective guilt over slavery and discrimination that they're willing to grant blacks a little bit of revenge. But only so long as this vengeance affects only white inmates and not themselves!

There it is again: the slavery that simply cannot be exorcised from the heads of blacks or whites.

I greatly enjoy my conversations with Mrs. Jefferson, because my life is quite lonely, and—in spite of those complications—she's more interesting to talk to than virtually anyone else I encounter on my daily travels around Brunswick. Think back on my day so far: with whom else could I have had a conversation about the University of California study described in the *Washington Post*? And the same goes for Mrs. Jefferson: with which other white prisoner or white guard could she have had a discussion about racism in corrections *and* her daughter's love life?

That such peculiar friendships between inmates and guards occur again and again is unavoidable. Nonetheless, what Mrs. Jefferson and I experience as a pleasant little diversion from our daily routine the Department of Corrections headquarters in Richmond sees as a security risk, something that must be combated at all cost. Richmond's latest tactic is, in the official jargon of corrections, to order that prisoners may no longer be referred to as "inmates" but must be called "offenders."

It's a fact that the prison bureaucracy produces an absurd amount of correspondence, written announcements, rules for guards and prisoners, posted memoranda, regulations, signs, and so on. For decades we've been known without exception as "inmates" in all of these documents. You'll observe that the word "inmate" is neutral in meaning. It merely denotes that the person is housed in a closed institution, but it says nothing about guilt or innocence. Some clever functionary at DOC headquarters in Richmond must have noticed this and thought to himself: *What a wonderful opportunity for a bit of psychological warfare!* The word "offender" very clearly implies *bad* and so serves as a constant reminder to both guards and prisoners that we're not to be trusted and that we deserve any mistreatment inflicted on us.

To make sure that everyone gets that message, every single rule book throughout the entire DOC was collected and replaced—as well as all regulations, posted memoranda, and so on. There were no substantive changes to the rules or regulations. In almost all cases, the only change involved replacing the word "inmate" with "offender."

Now the Departmental Operating Procedure says, "Every *offender* receives one roll of toilet paper per week." All day long, you hear or read this word. *What's on the offender menu for lunch? All offenders with appointments for the infirmary may now be released! Attention, attention, the offender library will be closed again this afternoon!* The more this terminology eats its way into the subconscious of corrections personnel, the more difficult it is for them to treat prisoners humanely, much less be friendly toward them. After all, offenders are *bad*!

This systemic destruction of human relationships also influences my little friendship with Mrs. Jefferson, my favorite guard. Should I ever attempt to escape, she wouldn't hesitate to fire a bullet into my back. During every conversation with her there hangs in the air between us the fact that, in an emergency, her duty is to kill me. And she will perform her duty admirably. She learned how to shoot extremely well in Chicago.

Perhaps that's why she only ever calls me by my last name, as she does with all of the other prisoners. I always address her as "Mrs. Jefferson," in the same way I do with all of the other guards. When it comes down to it, she's a human being, and I'm no more than subhuman.

Or, to use her terminology, she is white and I am black.

11:20 A.M.

After my conversation with Mrs. Jefferson has ended, I return to my cell. It's twenty past eleven and almost time to be counted again. My cell partner is already dozing on his bed, so I shut the door and sit in the gray plastic chair. The second meditation period of the day begins—a prison break that not even Mrs. Jefferson can stop.

You might wonder why I bother with meditation. My answer is that meditation leads to freedom—*real* freedom, not merely a multitude of freely choosable options. It's a good and pleasant thing to be able to select between Mercedes, BMW, and Porsche—one size does *not* fit all! But even in the outside world, a plethora of possibilities doesn't necessarily amount to true freedom.

No matter how many alluring options the world offers, we're still locked away in the prison of the self. All day long we listen to our own internal chatter, getting lost in the never-ending whirlpool of thoughts that swirl around the same things: sex and food, who I love and who I hate, the great idea about maximizing profits that I'm going to present to the board tomorrow. All of that together, so we believe, is our "self."

We are wrong. At its heart, meditation is a technique that allows us to examine all of the ideas we have about ourselves—calmly, quietly, and peacefully. What we come to see, or rather learn, is that none of these ideas about ourselves is really true.

I am not my body, although its urges, drives, and pains can

sometimes seem overwhelming. Nor am I my feelings—not even the euphoria of love or the anger that will not let go of me. I'm also not the noisy, swarming beehive of my constantly buzzing thoughts and ideas, no matter how proud of them I may be. They might perhaps prove my existence—*cogito ergo sum*—but they don't constitute a "self" by any stretch of the imagination. I know this because all of my urges, feelings, and ideas change from second to second. Everything dissolves and passes away and disappears. The "self" that existed just a moment ago has already vanished, never to return again. Nothing remains.

Through meditation, one learns to cease clinging to false concepts of the "self"; all of the urges, feelings, and ideas are allowed simply to pass by. If you practice this letting-go long enough, you eventually reach an open, clear space in which you can experience your own bare existence—one without a body, without emotion, without thought forms—as well as, at least sometimes, the presence of the truly Eternal, Good, and True. If you remain still in this open, clear space, absolutely and perfectly still . . . well, occasionally the self melts into the Eternal, Good, and True. *Not* in such a way that the self is somehow dissolved and lost, but rather in a manner that somehow respects the bare essence of the self as "self," even as it enters into union with the Eternal, Good, and True.

That's when you realize that, in this open, clear space, you were *always* in union with the Eternal, Good, and True. Here is your *true* home, the home which you'd never left, but which you couldn't see for a long time because you'd been sitting in the prison of the self.

As you might imagine, it takes frequent and regular practice to reach this open, clear space. On the way, you receive occasional glimpses of it, and each day the experience of freedom grows. With each meditation period, you free yourself a little bit more from all of the illusions you'd falsely identified as your self. You're finally able to deal with reality, instead of building and maintaining all those barred windows and walls and fences to protect yourself from the world.

I can only imagine how unimaginably difficult it must be in the outside world to find the time and motivation to even attempt the long-term project of self-liberation through meditation. I'm certain that I wouldn't have been able to do it had I not been incarcerated—if I'd finished my university studies and embarked upon a successful career. Only prison has given me the liberty to try to break out of the prison of the self. I had to lose my outer freedom in order to find my inner freedom.

At this point, however, I must emphasize that these two kinds of freedom should never be confused—which is what some well-meaning folks do when they try to comfort me with the thought that I'm freer in prison than most people in the outside world. Anyone who believes *that* may perhaps understand the nature of meditation very well, but they haven't a clue about life behind bars.

My inner freedom enables me to come to terms with the reality of my lack of outer freedom *without any illusions*. The inner freedom dispels the usual wishful thinking, self-deception, or projections of the self. But meditation is *not* an escape from the terrible reality of drugs, alcohol, homosexual rape, and all the other distractions of prison life. Quite the contrary. Through meditation, I'm given the freedom to face myself and to look the reality of my life straight in the eye.

Meditation allows me to say, *I live in Brunswick Correctional Center—not in the past, not in the future, but in the present, here in prison. There's no need to pretend: in this life, I have neither enough toilet paper, nor true friends, nor books in my native tongue. But I do have this day, these twenty-four hours. What shall I do with them?*

12:00 P.M.

At noon we're again allowed out of our cells because it's time for lunch. Instead of the five housing units being called one after another to the dining hall as they were at breakfast, the students from each building are called first so they may return to their classes as soon as possible. Many of the prisoners who live in the honor building are employed as teachers' aides, and when they're called to the dining hall along with the students, I simply slip out with them.

There's your proof: that awful Soering is still not rehabilitated. He still can't follow the rules! To this accusation, however, I have an answer: in my world, rules have an entirely different function than laws do in yours. In the outside world, laws govern the behavior of members of society so they may live peacefully with one another. In prison, the rules are designed to enable guards to accuse any inmate of a rule violation at any time. We all know and must never forget that we're totally dependent upon the good will and whims of the guards. As in the Bible, so in the penitentiary: we cannot be saved by our own good works but only by the mercy of our lords.

To put that principle into practice, correctional administrators quite deliberately wrote the rules in such a way that they cannot be obeyed. For instance, each prisoner is allowed only three sets of underwear. However, in the summer heat of Virginia, you have to change your sweaty clothes two or three times a day. Sometimes, guards will actively encourage inmates to break the rules and, thus, bring them under their power.

Take sex, for example: according to anonymous surveys, 44 to 65 percent of all prisoners are at least occasionally sexually active, but each sex act is a rule violation.[36] So what do the guards do? They allow "convict couples" to move into the same cell together as a reward for good behavior or for snitching.

Should the lovers ever get out of line, they'll appear before the Adjustment Committee (a sort of informal prison court) for infraction of Rule 209: "Engaging in sexual acts with others by consent." (This is in contrast to Rule 106(b): "Sexual assault upon or making forcible sexual advances toward an offender.") The penalty for violating Rule 209 is up to thirty days in punitive segregation. To avoid this punishment and to ensure continued access to their lovers, many homosexuals become reliable "employees" of the prison administration.

In this way, the irony of corrections becomes deadly. Hardly any better means of controlling the prison population exists than the capricious manipulation of Rule 209. The price of penitentiary peace is that tens of thousands of convicts across the nation are infected with the virus that causes AIDS. In the New York state corrections system, for example, 8.1 percent of the inmate population is HIV-positive.[37] The majority of these prisoners will one day be released, spreading a wave of infection throughout the civilian population. Just ask Mrs. Jefferson, my favorite guard.

Almost as bad as the physical corruption is the moral corrosion that occurs due to the deliberate manipulation of prison rules. It may be understandable and perhaps even necessary for the guards to maintain order in this way. Nonetheless, this method destroys whatever remnants of respect inmates may have had for the law. Over the years and decades, the guards drill into our heads that following the rules won't help us at all. But as long as we make nice with the guards and play the game like a good little lackey, we can do whatever we want. If this is the lesson we learn in the penitentiary, is it any wonder that so many released prisoners end up re-offending?

I don't have this last problem, since I'm going to croak behind bars anyway. So, you'll have to forgive me if today I again leave my housing unit too early to eat lunch with the students and the teachers' aides. I want to sit down with my friends at our regular table in the dining hall and have an enjoyable mealtime conversation. In my world, this little pleasure is worth breaking a rule for.

On the way from the hole in the wall where the trays emerge to the table where my friends are waiting, I collect oranges. We receive these precious golden globes of vitamin C only two times a week, so I panhandle for as many as I possibly can. I could get one of the kitchen workers to smuggle a small bag of oranges back to the housing unit for me. But that costs money, and I don't have much of that. So I beg instead, which is supposed to be good for the soul. How I wish that whoever invented that load of nonsense would try begging himself! To be blunt: poverty sucks.

Nowadays, however, we're all so poor—or rather, we receive so little food on our trays—that it's increasingly difficult to obtain extra oranges. Lunch today consists of a bread roll; a slice of bologna (made from the same turkey-and-soy mixture as everything else, but colored pink this time—which doesn't change the flavor at all); a very small, very thin slice of ersatz cheese (a three-and-a-half by three-and-a-half inch piece of yellowish congealed vegetable oil and soy, manufactured entirely without milk); one leaf of lettuce; a small dab of mustard; the usual one cup's worth of potatoes (this time diced and browned—half-burnt is better than raw); precisely half as much over-cooked spinach (which is really more of a green soup than anything else); and the aforementioned orange. In other words, we get a relatively good snack—for a twelve-year-old child. That's why today I'm only able to beg two additional oranges.

My lunch is spent with Richard, David, and Liam, who all live with me in the honor building and who are also not students or teachers' aides. All three of these guys perform rather important jobs and, thus, have official permission to go eat early. Richard and David work in the prison laundry, and Liam is the clerk for the prison-maintenance department.

Unlike me, these three spend six hours a day at their jobs. They'd happily labor even more, but because of the various count times throughout the day, working more than six hours isn't possible. Richard, David, and Liam work so hard because a job offers identity in a world where everything is the same; because work provides at least some meaning to our empty lives. For many inmates, the feeling of being totally useless is the worst punishment of all, so they're sincerely grateful if they're entrusted with important duties. Many turn into real workaholics and even suffer from job-related stress.

Liam is a perfect example of this type. In 1983, aged nineteen, he came to prison with a life-sentence for murder. Prior to that, he'd been in the navy, a typical farm boy from the Midwest: big, blond, and guileless. He'd wanted to cruise the world's oceans, but instead took a trip up the river. Like most young prisoners, Liam spent his first few years behind bars in shock, which led to the usual experimentation with drugs and alcohol. But then he got hit by the same lightning bolt that strikes many inmates after five or ten years: *If I don't start taking my life seriously, I'm never going to get out of here.*

This insight was still possible in the late 1980s, because at that time it was still possible to be granted early release on parole. That goal, that hope, that encouragement still existed.

Even lifers like Liam and me, and Harry and Richard and Sylvester and Eugene—all of us were officially told at our

Department of Corrections orientation sessions, "If you behave yourself, use your time well—learn a trade, get a degree—why, then you can expect to be released after fifteen to eighteen years."

From the standpoint of public safety this was and remains perfectly sensible. Only 20.6 percent of released lifers will re-offend, and just 3.7 percent will commit violent crimes. In contrast, 66.7 percent of released drug offenders will recidivate, and 12.3 percent of their crimes will be violent.[38] These numbers weren't known so precisely in the 1980s. But everyone in the law enforcement community was well aware that, paradoxically, lifers were the least dangerous category of parolees.

From Liam's point of view, the goal of turning his life around in hope of being released someday was entirely realistic. As his guide and guru he chose Benjamin Franklin, America's first and greatest Renaissance man. Scientist, inventor, author, farmer, businessman, diplomat, and politician, Franklin did it all. More than anyone else, Franklin embodied for Liam the idea that, in the Land of Opportunity, you really could achieve anything you wanted if you worked hard enough. Such a sentiment was no more and no less than the original American Dream of the self-made man, adapted for prison.

To make that dream come true, Liam devoured dozens of books—by Dale Carnegie, Norman Vincent Peale, and Og Mandino. The power of positive thinking became a kind of religion for him. With Liam, it was onwards and upwards; never, ever backwards. Liam soaked up whatever kind of knowledge was available and made it his own: from Tai Chi to cross stitch, from Spanish to calculus, from real estate investing to physics. He even taught himself to write solid, grammatically correct English, a skill that soon made him highly prized as a clerk. Almost in passing, Liam even completed an apprenticeship to become a fully qualified electrician.

His primary area of interest, however, was information technology. Though computers were still rare when he was arrested in 1983, Liam noticed even in prison that they were going to change the world. When the first computers began to show up in correctional facilities toward the end of the 1980s, Liam did everything possible to learn as much as he could about these miraculous machines. For an unofficial reward at his place of work, Liam never asked to steal anything but for more time on the computer. His parents sent him money—not to buy snacks to supplement the poor diet, but to purchase books on programming. On the recreation yard or in the dining hall, Liam exchanged tips and information with other inmates who'd fallen in love with computers, almost like other prisoners traded pornography.

Soon Liam found himself in the position of explaining to the civilian employees of the maintenance department just what these peculiar contraptions could do. In time, the plumbers, carpenters, metal workers, and electricians came to see him almost as an equal—a skilled colleague who could greatly lighten their workload. Word of Liam's abilities began to spread among the guards, too, and they started coming to him for advice as well. Recently, yet another grateful sergeant told him, "When you get out of here, you're going to be a millionaire!"

That is precisely what will almost certainly never happen.

In 1995, Virginia, like almost every other state, abolished early release on parole.[39] Inmates, such as Liam and myself, who were convicted before 1995, still have the right to a hearing before the board that makes parole decisions. But our applications for early release are routinely denied, and always for the same reason: "serious nature and circumstances of the crime." In the first half of 2006, for instance, only 2.9 percent of all eligible male prisoners were granted parole.[40] And the majority of those 2.9 percent had already served their entire sentences, so they received no more than a few months off the end of their terms. For those serving life sentences, there is no end. That is why Liam is quietly and unobtrusively cracking up.

Mental breakdowns are quite common in prison. In one way or another, virtually all prisoners with more than twenty years under their belts are psychologically damaged. A few years back, I knew an inmate who cleaned his entire cell every day—with a sponge that he constantly and carefully dipped *in the toilet*. This man was something of an exception, but many old timers in the corrections system have similar cleaning fetishes.

Some collect soap, hoarding forty or fifty bars or more and storing them on a shelf. Others "must" wash their clothes two or three times a day, or at least pay someone like Eugene to do it for them. Still others arrange every last object in their cells with extraordinary exactitude, lining up every item symmetrically at perfect right angles. I find all this completely understandable, since I too feel that prison life has dirtied me profoundly.

Almost as common as the soap collectors, washers, and organizers are those who spend the entire day in the infirmary waiting room. Because the nurses are massively overworked, they often interpret the complaints of these men as deliberate and malicious lies. A few convicts may be trying to run scams on nurses, but most of the prisoners I know who make regular trips to the infirmary are truly and sincerely concerned that what's causing them terrible pain is some life-threatening illness. And they're absolutely right. The life-threatening illness is called prison, and it is killing us slowly and painfully.

Many inmates steadfastly maintain that, before their incarceration, they were members of the CIA or some military special ops unit. So many of these guys can be found in penitentiary dorms and dayrooms that the rest of us have a standard joke about them: if only all these imprisoned spies and commandos had been sent to Iraq, the war would've been won long ago. These men aren't malicious liars but merely harmless nuts who believe their own fantasies. Like all people, they yearn for a better life, and since they've lost all hope in *this* life, they must resort to inventing a new one.

Liam, too, has begun to fall apart because of hopelessness. While he's no clean-freak or hypochondriac or CIA member, he . . . but no, I'd rather not tell you what kind of madness is eating its way into his brain. Liam isn't a literary invention, but a real person who's suffering terribly, and I don't want to put his pain on display. In any case, it's not as if anyone is going to come to his aid and alleviate his suffering!

What troubles me so much about Liam is not just that he's my friend, but that I see myself in him. Back when we still had serious conversations, we occasionally talked about how improbably lucky we'd both been. Somehow prison hadn't crushed us; somehow we'd actually become better people in this hell. He became a computer expert, and I a writer. Both of us, in our different ways, had even become amateur mystics. We really had no right to complain about prison, unlike the poor bastards all around us.

Now this God-forsaken place has destroyed even my friend Liam. And that scares me nearly to death. If even Liam—Benjamin Franklin's latter-day disciple, the dumb farm boy who managed to live his own American Dream even in prison—can crumble and crack up, then I can be crushed, too. I am no longer safe.

That's why I don't know what to say to Liam anymore. For several weeks I tried my best to find some way to stop his downward spiral. But we both occupy the same hole without an exit, that life sentence. I can't offer any hope to Liam, at least not without lying. Words are of no help to him. In my own helplessness, I've withdrawn from him. We still sit together at our usual table in the dining hall, but I don't try to have serious discussions with him anymore. I don't want to get infected. Whatever is crawling around in Liam's brain, it's not going to destroy me, too.

So Liam and I sit, eating our 61-cent lunch in Virginia's model prison, Brunswick Correctional Center. We obediently chew our pink turkey-and-soy bologna sandwich and exchange hardly a word. The American Dream has sputtered to a dead-end. But can anyone really live without a dream?

12:30 P.M.

Next to the dining hall exit is the gate that leads to the classrooms and the maintenance shop. Standing around the gate, waiting for it to open, are dozens of students and teacher's aides, smoking and chatting about sports. Here, Richard, David, Liam, and I part ways and head off to our respective jobs.

The model prison of Brunswick has more educational opportunities than most other correctional facilities in Virginia. But "more" is nowadays a relative term: Brunswick's 700 inmates have access to only two academic (GED) instructors, although 19 percent of prisoners cannot read or write, and a further 40 percent are functionally illiterate.[41] More than two-thirds of all inmates do not possess a high school or GED diploma.[42]

Many states have cut back on their school programs for prisoners to save money. Oregon has almost eliminated its GED classes, and in Maryland the waiting list runs into the thousands.[43] Voters love these deprivations. Why use taxpayers' money to pamper felons?

In this regard, Brunswick Correctional Center is a ray of hope. In addition to the two academic classes, the facility provides one-year vocational courses in auto repair, auto upholstery, furniture upholstery, and basic computing skills. These classes have on average only ten to twelve students, since most inmates know that further education is of no use to them. Sixty percent of all released prisoners are still unemployed one year after their release.[44]

What touches me time and again is how many inmates truly want to learn and work, if only they were given a realistic hope of bettering their lives through education. A case in point: these days it's hard to find furniture repair shops in this country, which is why so few prisoners express an interest in that particular vocational course. Painters, however, are always in demand, and those who employ them aren't particularly interested in their rap sheets. A painter can pick up an easy couple of dollars even in prison. When the maintenance department in Brunswick recently advertised a couple of open positions for painters, they received 78 job applications—fully 11 percent of the facility's population.

Many inmates have particularly severe learning disabilities. I know several good guys, hard workers, who simply cannot pass the GED test. In two cases with which I'm personally familiar, these men have been studying for more than *twenty years* without success.

But these things cannot be said in the U.S. without someone immediately and energetically having to add: *Of course, the learning disabilities of these prisoners do not in any way excuse their crimes.* This zero-tolerance, "no-excuses" argument is what passes for socio-political discourse in this country. Even mental illness, ethnic origin, and drug addiction, one is forced to add, *do not excuse these crimes at all.* Is it really honest to say that such influences have absolutely nothing to do with crime? Don't they mitigate even the smallest fraction of guilt?

The "no-excuses" argument is repeated continuously in order to justify harsh and merciless criminal-justice policies and relieve society of its inconvenient duty to offer better educational opportunities, mental-health assistance, anti-discrimination programs, and drug-addiction treatment to its (mostly black) lower class. If you've convinced yourself that poorly performing schools, psychosis, racism, and substance abuse *do not excuse crime at all*, then you're under no obligation to spend precious taxpayer dollars on improving social services.

I already have my high school diploma. I could theoretically take a college correspondence course, but the program is so expensive that it far exceeds my ability to pay for it. Furthermore, as my caseworker told me a few years back: "You're serving a life sentence—why would you want to study anything?"

Walking by the school building on my way to the gym, I pass the "snitch bench" positioned in front of the administration building. The assistant warden is sitting on the bench, hearing confession as she does almost every day at this time. In front of her is a short line of inmates standing meekly and obediently with bowed heads.

The moniker "snitch bench" wasn't coined by prisoners but by the guards. It's not *other inmates* whom we're supposed to rat out at the bench. The assistant warden isn't interested in such petty gossip; she has her security personnel for that! This location involves a different sort of snitching: prisoners are supposed to tell the assistant warden whether the *guards* are performing their duties and following procedures.

Was the gym shut down again this weekend because a male and female guard were having hanky-panky in some out-of-the-way office? Has the new nurse gotten herself involved with a convict? Should the civilian staff member who runs the recreation department be subjected to a drug test? We inmates must relate these pieces of information to the assistant warden—if not at the "snitch bench," then later, during a private audience in her office. It's hardly any wonder that the guards hate the "snitch bench" so much.

We are presented with another irony of corrections: everyone is a guard and everyone is a snitch. The guards keep an eye on prisoners and report rule violations to the lieutenant in the Watch Office. We observe the security staff and inform on them to the assistant warden on her bench. She watches us and the guards, but she herself is under observation by the security staff, and is occasionally even snitched on to head-quarters in Richmond—especially when she's been "too soft" on the inmates!

Everybody plays this game with a high degree of cynicism, because we all know how corrupt and morally corrosive it is. Nevertheless we continue to do it, selling our souls over and over again. Why we do so and how it happened that the entire prison became filled with guards, the guarded, and the snitches is a fascinating story that explains a great deal about life behind bars in the new millennium.

When I began my sentence at the end of the 1980s, the hope that we would one day be free kept us inmates under control. If you behaved yourself, you were released early on parole; if you didn't, you were incarcerated for longer. That system worked fairly well. In the mid-1990s, early release on parole was abolished, so a new means of control had to be invented, one that is now utilized in almost every state in the U.S. Each correctional facility receives a security-level designation from "one" to "six," with "one" being the least restrictive. Instead of the hope of freedom keeping us on a leash, we prisoners are given a simple choice: misbehave and get sent to a level six—the supermax—or play by the rules and end up in a pleasanter, lower-level prison.

The system is complicated by the fact that a security-level one penitentiary is not necessarily better than the others. None of the inmates at a level one or two facility has a cell. Instead, prisoners are housed in an enormous, open dormitory, where up to ninety-eight men are crammed together like sardines. Privacy is non-existent. The bunk beds stand in long rows directly next to each other; and two urinals, four toilets, and six showers are located in the open. When you wipe your behind, ninety-seven men and two female guards cheer you on. All night, inmates are playing card games in the aisles between the beds, and the TV pumps out loud rap-music videos, courtesy of BET®.

These dormitories are so insufferable that an acquaintance of mine even threatened to physically attack a guard, just so he could be transferred to a higher-level prison—one with cells. All his threats got him was a stint in punitive segregation.

The best correctional facilities in Virginia are not the security-level one or two dormitory prisons, but a facility like Brunswick, which has the unusual designation of 2/3. Prisoners have cells and a bit of privacy, and one can even buy little blue tickets for $1.50 in the prison store that you can exchange in the gym for a pint of ice cream. *Ice cream in prison*—that bit of news quickly made the rounds of the various correctional centers of Virginia. Not surprisingly, there are so many requests for transfers to Brunswick that the waiting list to get here is now almost two years long.

The irony of this situation proves once again that in order to control the behavior of human beings you need a heaven as well as a hell. The supermax is hell, of course—but who would have ever thought that heaven for prisoners would not be freedom, but just a better prison?

Once you arrive at the heaven of Brunswick Correctional Center, you realize you want to stay. So you go to the "snitch bench!"—everybody else does it!—and you play the game "guard–guarded–snitch" with the assistant warden, who is herself a perfect example of the second revolution in corrections that occurred over the last twenty or so years.

At about the same time as the security-level system was being developed, more women were being employed as guards and prison administrators. Brunswick Correctional Center has so thoroughly embraced this change that some housing units are now staffed exclusively by female correctional officers. The few male guards at Brunswick are mostly used as a "strike force"—the emergency tactical response team—which, since we're in heaven, is almost never needed.

The female officers serve as surrogate moms for the many young black inmates, the majority of whom were raised by single mothers. As you can imagine, these same women guards are also hotly desired sex objects. The perfect Freudian solution.

One can see convicts and female officers flirting openly all day and half the night in every housing unit dayroom at Brunswick. Even the plainest woman can feel like a celebrity in prison. Her fans will ply her with chocolates and sodas purchased from the Keefe store; in return, she can admire the muscles that her prison Romeos have worked so hard to perfect in the gym. When someone like me comes along and asks the guard to perform some facet of her duty—like opening the broom closet, perhaps—the lovebirds get seriously annoyed. I'm called a *player hater*, meaning that I'm trying to spoil a *player*'s amorous pursuit. In some cases, it's not at all clear who the *player* is: prisoner or officer.

A direct consequence of the much greater number of female guards is more safety. Every inmate knows without a doubt that half a dozen players will beat him to a pulp if he harms one hair on the head of the queen of the dayroom. In addition, the presence of women guards has undermined any possible solidarity among prisoners. The love-struck convicts have practically become honorary guards themselves.

The feminine method of control reaches its most sophisticated form in our assistant warden. She's white, which—let's be honest—enhances her authority and attractiveness, especially in the minds of the black prisoners. (If you have any doubts, ask Mrs. Jefferson about "slavery in the head.") She's always elegantly dressed in civilian clothes instead of the ugly, dark-blue uniform of the guards. As a matter of fact, she strongly reminds *me* of the mothers of my fellow students at the obscenely expensive private school I attended as a child. Such a lady engenders respect in every inmate, including me.

Cynicism aside, I much prefer doing my time in the heaven of Brunswick Correctional Center, where I'm kept on a leash by female security staff and $1.50 ice cream, than being locked away in the hell of the supermax, where male guards shoot at me. It may be a version of insanity, but I'm fully aware that, if I have to be in prison, then Brunswick is the best place to be. Nonetheless, I still find it somehow demeaning and dishonest to sell myself in this way.

One would assume that, ideally, Brunswick would be a place where prisoners do what's right because we *know* it's the right thing to do, and because we *want* to do right. I have the nagging feeling, however, that I do what's right only so I can stay in the heaven of Brunswick. Even the "nicest" penitentiary isn't a good thing; to the contrary, it's very bad. So I find myself in the peculiar position of doing the right thing in order to achieve something bad. There's something seriously wrong with this picture.

I've learned that, in case of doubt, you shut your eyes tight and push straight through. So I walk past the "snitch bench" once again, turn the corner, go through the gate to the rec yard, and then pass through the rear door of the gym. The guard is allowing the workers in to make a few preparations for the official opening of the gym in another fifteen minutes or so. However, I'm not here to clean toilets this time, but rather to play with the dogs.

Yes, the penitentiary has gone to the dogs.

My prison file says that I'm an especially dangerous sociopath, so incredibly intelligent that I'm able to manipulate even the most seasoned guard. At least, that's what a somewhat well-meaning lieutenant told me one time. I think there must be something to it!

As I step onto the large, open gym floor, I find about ten inmates, two female caseworkers in civilian clothes, and a slender young woman whose pants in the context of a men's correctional facility fit just a little too snugly. The group is standing in a circle in a corner and don't notice me as I slowly and stealthily sneak up on them.

I can feel my heart pounding faster and faster in my chest. They still haven't noticed me. I really *am* unbelievably clever and dangerous! Finally, I crouch down and whisper, "Nida, Nida!" And there she is, waddling her way between the legs of the other prisoners to stand right in front of me: a Sheltie—like a Collie, but only half as big. She's shy, but we already know each other. This is the third time she's allowed me to pet her, and it's not long before I'm in seventh heaven.

You may find this fuss over a little dog incomprehensible, but I've spent more than twenty years in a world without nature or any real, live animals. For many years, I had an unbelievably strong desire to touch the bark of a tree. When I shared my wish with an inmate named Don, he told me felt exactly the same way. Nida is much better than tree bark. She's a living, breathing creature who responds to my touch and leans into me as I scratch her behind the ears. I once stuck my nose into her plush coat, simply to smell something other than the penitentiary. In the few minutes I can spend with Nida I'm almost free.

Like everything else in prison, however, it's a big lie.

Nida and two other dogs—as well as the ten prisoners, two caseworkers, and the young woman with the exciting pants—are participants in the Pen Pals Program. During the next week, Brunswick is scheduled to introduce this program officially; what's occurring today is only a training session to prepare for the arrival of the Pen Pals dogs. These poor animals have been severely neglected and abused by their former owners and would otherwise be put to sleep. Through this program they can be brought into the facility to live in cells with model inmates in order to be trained and rehabilitated. The animals will then be placed with a loving family with children, and the next group of mistreated dogs will be brought into the penitentiary to be saved.

It sounds wonderful. And that's the whole idea behind the Pen Pals Program: it's good public relations. These kinds of programs are called "evidence based practices" by the corrections industry, and they're pure propaganda.

In the upper levels of the correctional bureaucracy, the leadership is well aware that the prison system cannot withstand concerted criticism. A recidivism rate of 67.5 percent says it all, and increasing numbers of citizens are demanding improvement in this area in particular. Except no one is willing to pay for it.

In the last chapter, I mentioned that 59 percent of all prisoners are either fully or functionally illiterate. Obviously, the recidivism rate cannot be reduced until these people are taught to read and write at least well enough to fill out a job application. In Virginia alone this would entail finding the resources to place special-education teachers in small classrooms with many computers *for approximately 20,000 inmates*. My own quick reckoning indicates that such a program would cost around $170 million per year. Taxpayers and voters aren't going to agree to this.

The despairing correctional bureaucrats are caught. On the one hand, they're supposed to lower the recidivism rate as quickly as possible; on the other, they don't have the money to do it. The answer is a Potemkin "evidence based practice" program such as Pen Pals. Or a softball league comprised of wheelchair-bound, elderly inmates who play against local clubs. Or a program to enable incarcerated mothers to visit with their children via web camera and the Internet. All these programs and more are available in Virginia and other states around the U.S.

"Evidence Based Practice" programs all follow the same pattern:

Exceedingly few participants. Only ten of Brunswick's 700 prisoners are allowed to take part in the Pen Pals Program.

Shifting program costs onto charitable organizations. An animal protection group pays for everything associated with the dog program—even the trainer with the great-fitting pants.

No meaningful or practical training. The inmate participants of the Pen Pals Program will eventually receive some kind of certificate. But what released prisoner can really earn a living wage as a dog trainer? An apprenticeship as a plumber, brick mason, or electrician would be much more practical, but no animal lovers have proved willing to pay for such programs.

A great deal of PR. The *real* purpose of "evidence based practice" programs is to (mis)lead the general public into believing that the prison industry is valiantly striving to rehabilitate the wretched villains. This is why these programs are always directed at the heart: the cute dogs, the nice old jailbirds in wheelchairs, the darling children and their sobbing inmate moms. Virginia newspapers frequently run stories about the Pen Pals Program in other correctional centers. But you will search in vain for one detailed report about the lack of genuine training and education for prisoners.[45]

The dog program illustrates the last point especially ironically. First of all is the fact—much discussed among inmates—that the dog food costs more than our 61-cent meals. We're therefore not only subhuman but even subcanine. But the irony goes still deeper. The stated purpose of Pen Pals is to rehabilitate and resocialize abused dogs so they can leave the facility restored and able to live with a good family in civilian society. The program proves that rehabilitation behind bars *can* actually work—at least for dogs. The obvious question is why the corrections industry doesn't rehabilitate us subcanines as well.

Because I know the answer to this question, I won't take part in the Pen Pals Program. I had originally submitted an application, but then withdrew it. I love Nida, but I simply can't allow myself to be exploited by the prison system for their propaganda.

Nevertheless, I can't rightly blame inmates who've chosen to participate in the program. I know them all, and some are even acquaintances. Like me, they've spent decades without any contact with nature or any opportunity to love a living being. I believe that the dog trainer from the animal protection group genuinely wants to help both the men and the animals, so I don't blame her, either. All are simply victims of the corrections department hierarchy in Richmond. By manipulating these people's affection for animals, the powers-that-be have turned these dog lovers into useful dupes, bit players in a public relations campaign to promote, in essence, kennels for humans.

I say goodbye to the beautiful little dog and sneak away

from the group in the gym. All of them are spellbound by the animals and take no notice of whatever else may be happening around them—like my little visit. That's fine by me, since I am now on my way to the law library to prepare for the Grand Revolution.

1:00 P.M.

Part One

Shortly before one, the guard opens up the front door of the gym. I slip past him and walk through the door immediately to the left that leads to the library on the second floor.

Every time I climb these stairs I can't help but be reminded that the stairwell was once a popular site for quick oral sex, in those halcyon days before surveillance cameras were installed. If you happen to stumble across one of these love scenes, you can't easily forget it. In fact, almost every corner of this prison carries a memory of that sort. No matter where you go, you're reliving some sordid, sad, or scary event.

The fence directly across from the doors to the gym and the library is where an acquaintance, David, tried to hang himself last year, shortly before Christmas. He must have thought that the guard on the rec yard couldn't see from his post into the corner where the fence and the building meet. But the razor wire on top of the fence must have shaken a little too much and, thus, warned the officer that something wasn't right. Whatever the reason, the guard found David while his legs were still kicking.

It's highly probable that several inmates observed David trying to hang himself. No one reported it because they would have violated the convict code, the iron rule of silence. Whether it's oral sex in the stairwell, a fight, or even a man trying to take his own life . . . *there ain't nothin' happenin' here, boy, so just walk on by and keep your mouth shut.*

The officer managed to get David down from the fence before he killed himself, but David still wound up brain dead. This is what I've heard, but prison is so filled with rumors that you can't ever be sure what the truth is. We never saw David again, unlike another guy who tried to cut his own throat. It's said that David was depressed because he'd been raped several times at another facility. I can't vouch for that, since that could just be pure rumor, too. It's a well-known fact that all prisoners are liars—especially sociopathic manipulators like me.

After climbing the stairs, I reach the library. It's been shut for the past several months because several inmates let themselves get caught with pornography. As soon as the inmates landed in punitive segregation, they went wild trying to out-snitch each other. They all wanted to remain in the heaven of Brunswick. It quickly emerged that a well-organized, highly lucrative pornography rental business had been operating out of the library. Keefe and MCI aren't the only ones who squeeze a profit out of correctional facilities.

The worst part for the administration was that the prisoners had apparently once again succeeded in corrupting some guards. Who else, other than correctional officers, could have possibly smuggled in relatively large items such as porn magazines and DVDs?

An offense so egregious demands harsh punishment! The library was closed down, supposedly so a few bookshelves could be rearranged and shortened to make it easier to discover porn-lending operations in future. Even though the remodeling was completed a couple of months ago, the library remains shut—an especially cruel blow in a world where, for many people, reading is the only means of passing the time apart from watching television. But it's vital to appear to be "tough on crime." Whether it's drugs in the outside world or pornography in prison, the small user gets hammered while the big dealer—or, in this case, the porn-smuggling guard—gets off scot-free. We see a uniformed smuggler prancing around the compound every day, soon to prance his way right into retirement.

I walk through the officially closed library until I reach a small, windowless room in the far back corner: the law library. This room can't be shut down, because it's where inmates prepare their lawsuits and appeals briefs. I've come here today to work on my own project, since (surprisingly enough!) I find cleaning the toilets in the gym insufficiently fulfilling or meaningful. As I've already suggested, I'm in the law library preparing the Grand Revolution.

I find good ol' Willy, who's fighting the same war as I am, albeit on a different front. He belongs to that species of man that's devolving from *Homo sapiens* to walrus. He's got a fat belly and a waddling gate, a thick gray mustache and big, chubby cheeks that make him look as if he's always on the verge of issuing forth an enormous snort or grunt. The law library is Willy's workplace and he spends as much time here as he can.

Willy's job is to assist other prisoners with preparing their lawsuits and court appeals. To help him, the administration coughed up a computer loaded with Virginia and U.S. statutes and case law. It's not a bad system and it's infinitely cheaper than providing full-time court-appointed attorneys for this prison's inmates, much less the 35,000 prisoners across the entire state.

Instead of a real lawyer, we get Willy: a nice guy, but an absolute layman, who also happens to be lacking in the grammar department. This is quite intentional. In every correctional center, the administration always carefully selects the inmates who work as clerks in the law library. Without exception, they're deficient in some fashion in reading and writing. It's not as if better qualified candidates can't be found. At Brunswick Correctional Center, for example, the administration could have hired Larry, a former professor of political science at a renowned state university. But he could have become dangerous in the law library, so instead of drafting legal briefs he's screwing chairs together in the prison's woodshop—much like me, a prize-winning author who cleans toilets in the gym.[46]

With Willy, however, the administration made a small miscalculation. It's true that his grammar isn't the best, but in spite of that challenge he's managed to educate himself (through correspondence courses at his own expense) to the point where he's able to actually help other prisoners. This makes him unique among law library clerks. As a result, I consider him my friend and comrade-in-arms in our struggle against the Leviathan of the criminal-(in)justice system.

You'd think that prison law libraries would be overflowing with guys like Willy and me, fighting the corrections system in any way possible. Who, after all, doesn't want to be free? But almost everyone gave up the struggle long ago and so Willy is once again entirely alone in the library as I walk in. Perhaps the other inmates simply have a more realistic grasp of the situation than we do.

The fact is that more than 90 percent of all prisoners pled guilty in court. These people have virtually no possibility of appealing their convictions, so Willy can't help them at all. Incidentally, the fact that the vast majority of all defendants plead guilty in court refutes the myth that all inmates are constantly whining about their innocence. As with most conventional wisdom and popular prejudice concerning the criminal-justice system, this one is also entirely false. Why do even those who don't challenge their guilt still complain? Rather than try to explain that to you, I'll provide you with a few examples that will allow you to observe the legal system through the eyes of the criminals and prisoners.

Let's begin with the case of my good friend Tex. When Tex's girlfriend became pregnant, she and her mother attempted to sell the unborn child: an adoption in exchange for a great deal of money. Tex flipped out, drove to the house of his girlfriend's mother, and stabbed her to death. He then attempted to commit suicide at the scene of the crime.

Tex was guilty, without a doubt. For second-degree murder, Tex received the minimum sentence of five years, of which he would actually have to serve four and a half. Even Tex found that to be relatively just: selling a baby is no excuse for killing someone.

Unfortunately, that isn't the end of the tale. When Tex arrived at his girlfriend's mother's house with a knife in his hand, he kicked in the door. In Virginia, the latter action meets the statutory definition of "breaking and entering with a deadly weapon." For this crime, Tex also received the minimum sentence: twenty years, of which he must serve approximately eighteen. Because the judge felt some compassion for Tex, he allowed the five years for the second-degree-murder conviction to be combined with the twenty years for breaking-and-entering. So Tex must now serve "only" eighteen years instead of a potential twenty-two and a half. This is what passes for leniency in Virginia. Tex calls it crazy and whines about the injustice of the legal system, even though he pled guilty in court.

Can you really blame him?

Of the less than 10 percent of all inmates who dispute their guilt, you might expect them to whine all the time. However, many of these criminals actually admit to being at least partially guilty—just not as completely guilty as the prosecutors claim. An example of this type of felon is my friend Carlton, a black inmate who today works as a clerk for the prison chaplain. What brought him here was a night of wild drinking followed by an automobile accident in which three people died. Since the prosecutor charged him with three counts of aggravated manslaughter, Carlton chose to go to court—not to challenge his guilt in and of itself, but the special, aggravating circumstances. Because of that decision, Carlton was slapped with a sentence of thirty years, of which he will end up serving approximately twenty-seven.

Can you blame him for whining?

Finally, there are those prisoners who maintain their complete innocence. In my experience, they account for at most two to three percent of all inmates. Indeed, according to a 2004 study conducted by Professor Stephen A. Drizzin of Northwestern University and Professor Richard A. Leo of the University of California, Berkeley, 28,500 prisoners are innocent.[47] At the time of the study, the population of U.S. corrections was 2.2 million, so this would suggest that 1.3 percent of all inmates are not guilty of their crimes.

I happen to know some of these people: one of them was my cell partner during the 1990s. His stepdaughter had accused him in 1991 of having sexually abused her one time in 1981. Since the supposed incident had occurred so many years earlier, there was neither forensic nor any eyewitness evidence available. But all the state of Virginia requires for conviction in a crime of this sort is a simple statement by the victim. On that basis, my friend was sentenced to fifty years in prison.

A few years later, my friend received a number of letters from the customers of the hair salon operated by his stepdaughter and his ex-wife. These customers were absolutely horrified because the two women had bragged while they were cutting hair that they'd deliberately set my friend up. His real crime was that he'd failed to send the ex-wife her alimony payment on time, so she'd wanted to get revenge. The local police eventually caught wind of what the two women were saying and called the stepdaughter in for questioning. She denied everything.

Unfortunately, no one can help my friend. Appeals courts these days aren't interested in claims of innocence if you can't produce any DNA evidence. Even the Innocence Project, co-founded by Barry Scheck and Peter Neufeld, will only help prisoners whose cases include DNA-based evidence. As in my friend's situation, the large majority of criminal cases don't have any sort of DNA evidence. For people like him, DNA testing, the so-called miracle of innocence, has turned into a permanent obstacle for vindicating himself.

Shouldn't he whine just a little bit?

Some may feel that it's entirely unimportant what inmates such as Tex, Carlton, and my friend think about the criminal-justice system. After all, Tex is a murderer, Carlton a drunk driver, and my friend an alleged child molester. But one of the declared purposes of the legal system is to teach villains respect for law and order—and it's in exactly this respect that the system has catastrophically failed. What inmates have learned instead is that *might makes right*.

Given this knowledge, it shouldn't be a surprise that when prisoners are released from the penitentiary, they take the lessons they've learned *from the authorities* about power—and the shoe will then be on the other foot. Violent crime in metropolitan areas has climbed steadily since 2005. Many criminologists think that just-released prisoners are contributing substantially to this trend.[48]

While we inmates wait for freedom, we aren't going to waste our time fighting for justice in the courts. My observation that the (in)justice system is buttressed by might making right is one shared by prisoners, and it's the reason why Willy sits by himself in the law library. In a sense, Willy is the last of the idealists in corrections, the only inmate who still believes that appeals briefs and lawsuits have some chance of success, however small. Because he can occasionally celebrate a tiny, partial victory, this belief lives on.

For many years, I, too, believed that justice was possible, that the appeals courts would in the end come to my rescue. That belief died in 2001—and that's when I began my career as an author and a revolutionary.

Part Two

In January 2001, the highest court in the land, the U.S. Supreme Court, decided that it wouldn't hear my appeal. With that, my whole purpose for living died. Since my arrest in April 1986, I'd lived for the day when justice would be done and I'd be set free. During all of those years, I fell into complete and utter despair only once, when, on the night of June 21, 1990 (the day of my conviction), I tried to suffocate myself with a plastic trash bag. Other than that, I'd never lost faith that one day I would finally be vindicated at the highest levels of the justice system. Now this dream was suddenly and irrevocably gone.

As if that weren't bad enough, my father and I had a falling out very shortly after the U.S. Supreme Court's decision. The denial of my last appeal was a terrible blow for him, too, since he'd organized and financed the fifteen-year legal battle. My guess is that he'd had enough and seized the first opportunity to break from me.

Because my mother had died in 1997, I now found myself completely naked in the world. I had no reason for living, no family, and no prospect for freedom. My contact with the outside world consisted of two friends: an American pastor and a high school pal who'd meanwhile moved to England. Otherwise, I had only my meditation and my prison job in the gym.

For about a week I played around with the idea of killing

91

myself, going so far as to ask around for a needle and heroin. I had just enough money left for one golden shot to end my misery. But I decided that I would first write a book about meditation. There'd be enough time to commit suicide later.

I realized that my prospects for getting the book published were slim to non-existent. In fact, in the 1990s I'd written a "true crime" book about my trial, as well as a John Grisham–style novel, and I'd been unable to find a publisher for either. A book about meditation, and by a prisoner no less, seemed something that would have no chance of being published, let alone selling. Yet I wrote the book anyway.

In one respect, writing the book was a way of avoiding death by suicide. But seeking an escape wasn't the only reason for working on it. Something I didn't understand and couldn't explain drew me to the project. Two thousand and one turned into a year of blind faith and trust. As the book took shape, it seemed as if it came alive even before it was born. After its birth, it would continue to have a life of its own.

I wrote in the prison visiting room. At that time, I wasn't only the toilet cleaner for the gym but also the photographer in the visiting room. For a $1.50 ticket bought in the prison store, inmates could have a picture taken with their visitors.

It happened there were relatively few customers for photos, and so I could spend the otherwise empty hours working on the book. I was atypical, since visiting-room photographers usually spend their time flirting with the mothers, sisters, and daughters of other prisoners. No one had ever seen a photographer who didn't try to chat up female visitors in the visiting room before!

Word of this strange new phenomenon soon spread. In time, the guards in the visiting room became quite friendly, and the inmates were grateful I wasn't constantly attempting to look up the skirts of their womenfolk. As everyone finally came round to the idea that I was different, some regular visitors even started buying me food from the vending machines and asking me what I was writing so feverishly at my little table.

At the end of 2001, my book was finally ready. I gave the manuscript to the mother of one of my fellow prisoners (one who had been feeding me out of the machines), and she sent photocopies to more than a dozen publishers. Naturally, none of them accepted the book; in fact, most didn't even bother to reply.

But the lady who mailed out those manuscripts to publishers also sent a copy to Thomas Keating, the co-founder of Contemplative Outreach, and a popularizer of the form of meditation—centering prayer—that I practice. By some miracle, Fr. Keating read the book and forwarded it to one of his publishers, Gene Gollogly of Lantern Books. In the fall of 2002 the contract was signed and a year later *The Way of the Prisoner* was on the market. With that, I reached the goal I'd set in 2001. The book project now completed, I could finally commit suicide. In the meantime, however, the context of my entire life had changed.

Even before *The Way of the Prisoner* was published, photocopies of the manuscript were making their way into the hands of all kinds of people. I suddenly found I had a small circle of friends and supporters, and the more people read the manuscript, the more that circle grew. In a funny sort of way, I'd written myself into a trap.

In *The Way of the Prisoner* I praised centering prayer as being a virtual life-saver. If I were to do myself in now, then I'd be proving the exact opposite. The book would be taken off the market and all my hard work would have been for naught. On top of all that, my publisher began urging me to put into practice the message of *The Way of the Prisoner*. This book claimed that meditation can enable you to transform life's tragedies into something positive by finding a way to help others *through* your own suffering. As an example, I cited my own life: prison had turned out to be a blessing because it had brought me meditation, and now I was able to pass on the gift of inner silence to my readers through my book.

My friends at Lantern were of the opinion that this wasn't enough—that I'd essentially obligated myself to also help my fellow inmates. So the fall of 2004 saw the appearance of my second book, *An Expensive Way to Make Bad People Worse*. This was my attempt to explain to conservatives why the corrections system is nothing more than another government boondoggle, an enormous waste of money that achieves nothing. The most important cornerstones of my argument were as follows:

In 1973 there were approximately 300,000 prisoners in the U.S., and by 2003 there were around 2.1 million.[49]

The crime rate in 2003 was exactly the same as in 1973.[50]

In other words, America was spending seven times as much money on prisons as thirty years previously, without the slightest improvement in public safety. *That* is a clear case of defrauding the taxpayer.

(This argument is not at all weakened by the fact that, in 2005 and 2006, the number of violent crimes increased in some metropolitan areas. During that time frame the number of *non*-violent offenses fell sharply. Thus, the overall crime rate, which includes both violent *and* non-violent offenses, continued to decline throughout 2005 and 2006.[51])

Even before *An Expensive Way to Make Bad People Worse* was released, I'd almost completed my third. But *The Convict Christ* experienced . . . a little unforeseen delay. Exactly one week after a Richmond newspaper published a positive article about *Expensive*, I was thrown into punitive segregation.

1:00 P.M.

Part Three

I should've known that something wasn't right as soon as I saw a guard and a sergeant standing in front of my cell door (normally cell searches are conducted by two ordinary guards). What's more, it was lunchtime, whereas cell searches are usually done right after breakfast. Believe it or not, I was naïve enough to think nothing of it.

I also didn't connect the security personnel's visit in any way with the recent appearance of the newspaper article about *Expensive*. After all, the journalist had been so complimentary! The idea that public praise for my coolly presented and factually sound critique of the prison system would be regarded by corrections officials in Richmond as especially dangerous simply didn't occur to me. So with some equanimity I let the sergeant and guard put handcuffs on me and watched them as they rummaged through my belongings.

They found the floppy disk almost immediately, since I hadn't bothered to try to hide it. I hadn't thought it necessary. The staff member for whom I worked at that time had given me the disk explicitly for the purpose of storing the text of my third book about the convict Christ on it. At the time, I hadn't yet begun cleaning toilets in the gym but was instead employed as a clerk for the adjustment committee chairman. His job consisted of holding short hearings when an inmate had been accused of breaking a prison rule. I helped to organize the flood of forms and reports associated with those hearings, and for that task he'd given me an old computer.

As with all penitentiary jobs, this one, too, came with an unofficial reward to compensate for the paltry wages. Stealing office supplies to sell on the rec yard didn't interest me, but writing my books on the old computer certainly did. This activity was contingent upon two conditions: first, my boss, the adjustment committee chairman, had to personally read through everything I wrote; secondly, I was required to store everything on the floppy disk rather than the computer's hard drive.

When the sergeant and the guard found that floppy disk, I explained the circumstances and asked them to call my boss to confirm everything. The sergeant said that this is what he would do, and if I was telling the truth, he'd return the disk to my boss.

The handcuffs were taken off and the shakedown team disappeared. I wasn't worried, since at that time—2004—many prisoners were getting caught with computer disks without being formally charged with a rule violation. Only one week before this incident, in fact, an inmate by the name of Richie Y had been found in possession of a disk—and he didn't even have permission from his boss, the librarian, as I did. Yet Richie received no punishment at all.

What I'd overlooked, however, was that Richie's disk only had music on it, whereas mine contained a book that attacked the prison system.

With a calm soul and a quiet conscience I went to the dining hall, obediently ate my 61-cent meal, and returned to the housing unit. There I was met by the sergeant, who told me he'd received orders to throw me into punitive segregation. It was obvious that the poor man was embarrassed: he knew me and was very well aware that his superiors were playing a foul game with me. (This sergeant was the only participant in this little drama apart from myself who did *not* receive a promotion later on, which may or may not be a coincidence.)

I took a speedy trip to the "hole," as it's known among prisoners. I wasn't being accused of any rule violations (they even gave me that in writing!) but was instead only being placed "under investigation." Naturally, it was impossible for the powers-that-be to tell me why.

Apart from the fact that the authorities either could or would not tell me what I was supposed to have done, such investigations are not particularly unusual. Every correctional facility, including Brunswick, has a guard whose primary responsibility is to function as an institutional investigator. At the time of this event, the investigator's office was a windowless chamber next to the punitive seg. cells known as the "ice room." Inmates whose misdeeds were being looked into would be brought to the ice room in handcuffs and interrogated by the investigator. Astonishingly enough, the inmates always confessed—no one was ever innocent—and, thus, the investigator could conclude each and every one of his inquiries with a conviction.

I thought that something like this was now in store for me. Yet nothing happened. Although I ended up spending six weeks in the hole—an unusually long time, since the maximum punishment for a rule violation is thirty days—I never once saw the investigator. In fact, at no time was I ever interrogated, questioned, or even given a clue as to what was going on. The authorities had put me in the cooler, so to speak, and waited patiently for me to figure out that I'd have to confess to something or snitch on someone in order to leave the punitive seg. unit.

On my second day in the hole, I was taken to a hearing before the assistant warden. Two guards appeared at my cell door and opened the hatch through which they handed me my three daily meals. I had to stand with my back against the door, lean forward, and stick my hands through the hatch behind me. After the guards had handcuffed me, I was allowed to pull my hands back through the door and straighten up.

Then I had to walk over to my bed—all punishment cells are single cells—and kneel on it so that my feet and ankles were hanging over the edge. The door opened, the guards stepped in, and leg-irons were placed on my ankles. To assist me in getting off the bed with all those chains on me, the guards grabbed me by both arms and helped me stand.

It's not easy to walk in leg-irons. The two locks are on the inside of your ankles, so you have to swing your legs outward in a small semi-circle with each step to keep the locks from banging together. You acquire a rolling sailor's gait, except that you can't use your arms to help you balance, since they're handcuffed behind your back.

Then there's the dog leash running from the cuffs to the guards. I'll never forget how we prisoners laughed at the free-worlders when indignation erupted over the pictures of American soldiers leading around Iraqi prisoners on dog leashes at Abu Ghraib. *What's the big deal?* we all wondered. Dog leashes for human beings are standard equipment in every correctional institution in the United States. The U.S. Army Reserve soldier who was convicted of being ringleader at Abu Ghraib was a prison guard in Virginia, and another was a guard in Pennsylvania. Those boys were simply doing what they'd been trained to do in American penitentiaries.

I, too, found myself at the end of a dog leash, wobbling forward on shaky legs to attend my hearing before the assistant warden, the official purpose of which is to tell the inmate that he's been assigned to the segregation unit. You actually receive a form that says so.

Of course, the unofficial purpose of this hearing is something else entirely. As with the snitch bench, the hearing is the prisoner's opportunity to cough up useful information to the assistant warden, preferably some indiscretion or mis-demeanor by a staff member. For such valuable information, the inmate can receive a reduction in punishment or even an acquittal when he later appears before my boss, the adjust-ment committee chairman, for the official hearing.

Like all prisoners, I had some compromising information stored up in case of an emergency such as this. In fact, my job had given me unique access to especially useful material. But I had absolutely no idea of what I was supposed to have done. And I couldn't see why I should have to snitch in order to buy my way out of the hole for some sin that I couldn't even identify. So I denied all guilt at the hearing, didn't give any information to the assistant warden, and was promptly taken back to my seg. cell. With that began the six-week effort to grind me down.

This hadn't the slightest chance of succeeding. The punish-ment of the hole essentially consists of isolation. For twenty-three hours a day—twenty-four during the weekend—you remain in your cell, locked in and alone. You have no one to talk to, no one to play cards with, no TV to watch, and only three books a week to read (if you're lucky). For the majority of inmates, these conditions are unbearable; for me, they were perfect. In the hole I had more peace and quiet to meditate and write, my two favorite activities.

The poor guys in the cells surrounding mine were suffering terribly. Under the psychological pressure of almost complete isolation, the majority of prisoners break down quite quickly. Outsiders probably can't even imagine the effects of enforced solitude and idleness. But among corrections professionals, this phenomenon has been known for almost two hundred years.

The very first modern long-term prison in the world, the Eastern State Penitentiary, was built in 1829 in Cherry Hill, Pennsylvania—by the quiet, peaceful, benevolent Quakers, of all people. Under their "tough love" tutelage, the inmates were supposed to be led to repentance for their sins through isolation and forced meditation. But neither repentance nor meditation can be forced on the unwilling, and the prisoners at Cherry Hill soon lost their minds completely. The Quakers' grand experiment with correctional reform had to be abandoned almost as soon as it began.[52]

The prison bureaucracy forgets nothing, however, not even the failed experiment of Eastern State. Isolation may not be able to induce repentance—but as punishment, it's extremely effective. Consequently, from 1829 to the present, every penitentiary in the U.S. punishes unruly inmates by locking them in single cells in order to inflict severe psychological pain, the same kind of torture that drove the prisoners at Cherry Hill insane. When you observe this experience up close, as I did in the hole, you see (or hear) the same, near-psychotic reactions to the stress of isolation over and over again.

First of all are the "ramblers," inmates who have conversations with themselves for hours on end. They shout through the ventilation shaft or yell out of the window. They tell endless stories, even though no one is listening. Then come the "drummers," who monotonously beat on the metal tables all day long and especially at night. During my six weeks in the hole, however, I saw much more deranged behavior.

In the cell diagonally across from mine, a prisoner regularly "gunned down" the nurse on her morning rounds. He deliberately masturbated so that she'd see him through the cell door window as he ejaculated. Another man managed to acquire a piece of plastic, sharpened it on the cement floor, and then began digging into the flesh of his arm because he was certain there were "worms in there." Yet another inmate smeared his feces on the cell walls, which everyone throughout the entire hole could smell. No one committed suicide during my time in segregation, but that, too, happens on occasion. In fact, it occurred just last week.

To understand the significance of the hole and the psychoses it engenders, it's necessary to understand that none of these behaviors is exceptional. All the abnormal, deranged reactions of the prisoners in isolation have been planned for by the corrections bureaucracy. Far from viewing them as unusual emergencies to be avoided in future, prison staff prepare for them as a matter of routine, knowing full well that they'll happen again and again.

The Wallens Ridge supermax has an entire cell block designated for "gunners." Only male guards are allowed to work there, although that doesn't deter the "gunners" in the least. At Brunswick, the Mental Health Unit is about to start a special program for the "cutters," those who injure or mutilate themselves because they believe worms are crawling beneath their skin. In every hole across the land, guards wear special protective plastic suits when they have to extract a "shitter" from his feces-smeared cell.

To deal with the cutters, the shitters, and the potential suicides, every segregation unit has special cells outfitted with raised beds, upon which these inmates can be tied down by their arms and legs. This happened several times while I was in segregation. However, the U.S. Court of Appeals for the Fourth Circuit issued a decision in 2006 stating that authorities weren't permitted to use these so-called "five point restraints" for more than five consecutive periods of 46 to 48 hours each. Think about it: that's almost a ten-day stretch! In such a situation, said the court, the inmate must be granted a hearing.[53]

All of the gunners, cutters, and shitters get their hearing. Public masturbation, self-injury, and feces-smearing are all rule violations: numbers 210, 234, and 237 respectively. So when these psychologically damaged people are brought before the adjustment committee chairmen at their facilities, they receive even *more* time in the hole, which of course only increases their pathological behavior.

Punitive segregation units and the virtually identical super-max penitentiaries are becoming more widespread. Between 1996 and 2006, the number of prisoners who had to learn to survive under these conditions grew from 48,000 to 70,000.[54] The state of New York has calculated that it costs $16,000 less to house an inmate in a punitive segregation (or supermax) "S-Block" than in a normal facility.[55]

When prisoners are accused of being a member of an organized gang such as the Crips or the Bloods in states like California or Texas, they can end up spending decades in isolation. So far, Virginia hasn't reached that level of inhumanity, but when I was in the hole in 2004, I met up with a Rastafarian who'd been in punitive seg. continuously since 1999. That year, corrections officials in Richmond changed one of their policies once again. Effective immediately, all inmates had to cut their hair short, ostensibly for security reasons.

The fact that the religious tenets of the Rastafarians forbid them from cutting their dreadlocks interested the gentlemen in Richmond not at all. Thus, my friend Ras Talawa Tafari, as well as several dozen other Rastafarians and Muslims, found themselves in the hole. In time, many capitulated and others were released from prison. When I met Ras, he was one of only a handful of the faithful scattered amongst various correctional centers across Virginia.[56]

We were able to speak with each other five times a week. Mondays through Fridays, we were taken from our cells in handcuffs and allowed a short recreation period in the "dog cages," a cage about the size of a cell, but in the fresh air. What was more precious was that you were allowed to see and speak with other people for about an hour, from wire cage to wire cage.

I found the conversations with Ras very edifying. He practiced a different form of meditation than I did, but that didn't matter. Like Willy in the law library or me with my books, Ras had found the strength to survive through peaceful resistance against the Leviathan of corrections—or the "Babylon Beast," as he called it.

Of the three of us, Ras certainly has it the worst. Without thanks or recognition, he's allowed himself to this very day (I write these lines in 2007) to be psychologically tortured in the hole, for no other reason than that he wants to serve God in his own way. This hasn't driven Ras crazy, either, but has changed him into an uncommonly peaceful, friendly person. Even the guards in the hole like him, going so far as to give him an extra piece of fruit at lunch. You can read a long interview I conducted with him in my fourth book, *The Church of the Second Chance.*

Unlike Ras Talawa Tafari, I'm not a martyr. After approximately five weeks in punitive seg., I wrote a letter to the reporter whose article about my second book had presumably led to the cell search and the discovery of the floppy disk. This reporter then telephoned the headquarters of the Department of Corrections in Richmond and asked why I was cooling my heels in the hole. He didn't know anything about it, the DOC spokesperson told the reporter; if he called back the next day, perhaps more information would be available. Before the reporter could do so, I was released from segregation.

To this day, no one has offered me any reason or explanation as to why I was placed "under investigation." Shortly before the publication of my third book in the spring of 2006, a verbal message from a senior administrator of the Department of Corrections was relayed to me: I needn't fear any future difficulties because of my books. Let's see how long this peace will last.

I'm well aware that the book you're reading right now could provoke my transfer to another penitentiary: *If Soering finds the model prison Brunswick so distasteful, perhaps he belongs at a supermax!* It's also conceivable that I could be moved to one of those nightmarish level-two dormitories, and this could even be done as a "reward" for good behavior. When it comes to inflicting punishment, the prison bureaucracy is quite inventive and experienced, after all.

By way of taking some precautions against possible future retaliation, I'd like to conclude this chapter with a few comments about Alexander Solzhenitsyn, the author of *One Day in the Life of Ivan Denisovich*, from which I've borrowed the title for this book. In fact, the model for the text was not *Ivan Denisovich* but rather an entirely different work, his novel *The First Circle*.

The First Circle describes the most pleasant penitentiary in the entire Soviet Union, the model prison of the gulag system. In this facility, all the convicts were nuclear physicists convicted of pro-Western leanings and were treated so well that they continued to build atom bombs for Mother Russia even in captivity. Despite the many privileges and all of the little extras they received, the prisoners found their existence pure hell—albeit the first circle, an allusion to Dante's *Inferno*.

Brunswick Correctional Center is in many respects the counterpart to Solzhenitsyn's luxurious gulag. Perhaps it's *only* in relatively humane penitentiaries like these that you're able to see clearly that a cage remains always a cage, regardless of how "nice" the guards make it. The "humane prison" doesn't exist; the very idea is a contradiction in terms.

The powers-that-be in the Soviet Union showed little patience with such theorizing about human liberty. Solzhenitsyn was punished for *The First Circle*. I'll be interested to see if the correctional authorities of Virginia act any differently.

1:00 P.M.

Part Four

After I was released from punitive seg. toward the end of 2004, Gene Gollogly agented my third book to Orbis Books, a Catholic publisher, which published it in the spring of 2006. *The Convict Christ* connects scenes from penitentiary life with excerpts from the four gospels in which Jesus talks about prisoners and criminals. Jesus speaks about or with those like me fourteen times, from the very beginning of his ministry up to his crucifixion:

- In his very first public sermon, Jesus announced, "The Lord . . . has sent me to proclaim freedom for the prisoners" (Luke 4:18).
- At the end of his life, he was himself a prisoner: "Two other men, both criminals, were also led out with him to be executed" (Luke 23:32).

You'd think such a book would fly off the bookstore shelves in America, a land that claims to be especially religious. Unfortunately, that hasn't been the case, mainly because the majority of American Christians have a concept of God based on the Old Testament Yahweh, the Judge who metes out "hard but fair" punishment for every breach of his Ten Commandments. Americans, like all Christians, also believe in the love and mercy of God. But these attributes take the form of a transfer of well-deserved punishment from guilty sinners onto his own innocent Son on the Cross.

This theology is called "penal substitution," and its origins go back to the Italian Catholic St. Anselm (1033–1109) and the Swiss Protestant Jean Calvin (1509–1564). When the Puritans traveled to the New World, they took a simplified, pietistic version of "penal substitution" with them. Jonathan Edwards (1703–1758) turned it into a kind of national religion through his phenomenally popular sermon, "Sinners in the Hands of an Angry God." To this day, Edwards' sermon remains part of the standard theological arsenal in most seminaries and is widely distributed as a tract.

Conservative Christians openly and enthusiastically embrace this concept of an "angry" God who holds "sinners" in his vengeful "hands." At every opportunity, they speak joyfully of being "saved"—from hell, the just retribution of the divine Judge. A lightly camouflaged form of this same basic idea can be found among progressive Christians, too. They prefer to speak of the selfless love of Jesus, the God-Man who sacrificed himself for us; but they rarely question whether a God of Love would really demand such a bloody, fatal sacrifice. When I exchanged letters with the widely known progressive theologian Rev. Ronald J. Sider, he asked me rather defensively what was wrong with the concept of penal substitution.[57]

For me, this theological blind spot explains virtually everything wrong in American politics. No candidate can be elected to office without discussing his own religious faith at length and allowing himself to be regularly photographed as he attends church services. Once in power, he must then operationalize his religious worldview—one based on vengeance from the punitive God of "penal substitution" theology.

Thus, terrorist attacks require military retaliation—if necessary against a substitute target like Iraq. Under the "No Child Left Behind" law, poor test results call for the "hard but fair" punishment of schools and teachers in the form of budget cut-backs. In the judicial system, criminals are shown no mercy at all, as one can see especially well in the treatment of juvenile offenders. Only twelve youths outside of the U.S. are serving life sentences without the possibility of parole. Seven of them are in Israel, four in South Africa, and one in Tanzania. In the United States, no fewer than 2,200 juveniles are serving life sentences without any hope of one day being released.[58]

This staggeringly disproportionate figure cannot be explained by normal political or cultural differences. We are dealing here with something entirely different and much deeper—namely the relationship with and the understanding of God. If you take God seriously, you give him what he demands—and the angry American God, who holds sinners in his hands, demands punishment.

As far as I'm concerned, one has to grasp this socio-theological concept in order to appreciate American attitudes toward incarceration. The policies and decisions that I have described in these pages are not mistakes or well-intentioned but badly executed actions. It's also not as if Americans wouldn't be just as shocked by conditions at Brunswick as a European such as me. But I would suggest that very few Americans are likely to question the basic principle that punishment must be exacted and that it must be "hard but fair."

Perhaps surprisingly, I believe that the way out of this theologically inspired dead end is not increasing secularism, but a theological revolution, a new understanding of God. The U.S. has always been, and forever will be, a deeply religious country. Therefore, any transformation must take place from *within* this faith rather than as an attack *against* it. Among some conservative Christians—those who support "faith-based initiatives," for instance—one can already see signs of change.[59] My fourth book, *The Church of the Second Chance*, is addressed to these believers and their developing, growing faith.

Since there's no room in my cell for the mountain of research I conducted for *The Church of the Second Chance*, I've donated many of the studies and reports on the corrections system to Willy and his law library. Other inmates can now read them and continue their education in this area, if they want to. Only a very few will take advantage of this opportunity. The overwhelming majority of prisoners have simply given up trying to understand what's happened to them.

I've come here today because my editor Sarah has asked me to double-check some dates and figures for the endnotes of *The Church of the Second Chance*. I take special care of that kind of thing because I want to ensure I can document every assertion I make. Besides, I have some readers who read my books with a special care of their own.

Take Helen Fahey, for example, the chairperson of the five-member Virginia Parole Board. She has already told my advocates twice that she's read all of my books.[60] Mrs. Fahey knows that I've quoted her in Chapter 5 of my second book, Chapter 7 of my third, and Chapter 9 of my fourth. In all three cases I can cite exactly when and where she made these remarks.

Luckily, Mrs. Fahey does not take offense at my literary endeavors. Each time she denies my application for release on parole, she always gives the same reason: "serious nature and circumstances of the offense." Since the serious nature of the offense will never change, *ipso facto* I will never be released.

You shouldn't think, however, that such reasoning is a logical fallacy on Mrs. Fahey's part. She's not at all concerned with public safety. In my case, parole would lead to my immediate deportation to Germany, thereby removing any danger to the citizens of Virginia or indeed the United States forever. Nor is Mrs. Fahey particularly interested in rehabilitation. As far as I know, no other inmate has managed to have five of his books published, some to critical acclaim, as I have. Why do these things not matter to Mrs. Fahey? Because she is a Christian in the Jonathan Edwards tradition. She believes that God demands punishment—and not rehabilitation, public safety, or apparently even mercy.

As it happens, I am a Catholic, and relatively conservative to boot. Nothing that I write here should be construed as a criticism of Christianity *per se*, but only of what I believe to be the un-Christian concept of a judging, punishing God. I'm also not blaming Americans for the misbegotten theological concept of "penal substitution." After all, it originated with Anselm and Calvin in Europe, and more and more Americans are beginning to reject it. Many of my friends and readers of my books in this country are Christians of this latter type. The fact that *The Convict Christ* won a literary award in the summer of 2007 suggests that the punishing God of "penal substitution" is losing ground.

In place of Jonathan Edwards, Christians such as those mentioned above are embracing the ideas and writings of the German Protestant Dietrich Bonhoeffer (1906–1945) and the Dutch Catholic Henri Nouwen (1932–1996). Frankly, I doubt that most of my fellow Europeans would be as open to American theologians as many Americans are to Bonhoeffer and Nouwen.

This more enlightened Christian is still in the minority in this country. It will take many years for someone like Helen Fahey to read and absorb a book like Nouwen's masterpiece, *The Prodigal Son*. Until then, I will remain in the hands of an angry God—or, rather, in the hands of his self-appointed instruments on earth.

2:45 P.M.

The law library closes at a quarter to three. As is often the case,
I feel I haven't done enough today. On Mondays, Wednesdays,
and Fridays I have only the afternoons free for my writing:
mornings are devoted to cleaning toilets and lifting weights,
while evenings are spent leading a Tai Chi class—a further
part of my job in the gym that I describe in more detail later.
On Tuesdays, Thursdays, and Saturdays I work on my books
through the morning and run in the afternoon or evening.
Four or five hours of writing per day is all I can handle, since
this kind of work is surprisingly draining.

I leave the library, climb down the stairs, turn left, and cross
the rec yard to the gate leading to the housing units. From
each of the buildings, streams of inmates are flowing through
the sliding double doors: it's gate break. My path takes me past
the infirmary, where I run into Omo and L.A.

Although at first glance we have nothing in common, I've
become very fond of these two men. They're dinosaurs like
me, having served twenty to thirty years each. But Omo and
L.A. are black and in their late fifties, and some of their other
friends are the kind who hate whites on principle.

Both Omo and L. A. meditate regularly, though they use different approaches. Once a Muslim, Omo (he tells me his name
means "he who returns home" in an African tongue) is now
more a Buddhist than anything else, even though he's never
taken vows. L.A. was, and to some extent remains, a member
of the Nation of Islam. In contrast to some of his fellow believ-

ers, L.A. doesn't demonize whites. My feeling is that in many respects he's distanced himself from the Nation's party line. Both he and Omo are constantly reading books on meditation, regardless of whether they're from Buddhist, Christian, secular, or other perspectives.

In the meditation group I lead are several other older black men like Omo and L.A., although I don't know them as well. All of them were once known to be dangerous—real terrors of the cellblocks, "convicts" through and through. They are (or were) exactly the type of person whom even I would have argued would never be rehabilitated and should never be released.

Nonetheless, these "monsters" now sit in complete meditative silence for forty minutes without moving a muscle. Years and often decades have passed since their last rule violation, and religiously motivated hatred of whites no longer plays a role in their lives. When these men see me in the yard or elsewhere, they always greet me. Or, in the case of Omo and L.A., they give me the handclasp and one-armed embrace once reserved only for brothers in the faith.

It wasn't my little meditation group that caused this spiritual revolution, since the group only came into existence in 2005. In the spring of that year a pastor visited me after having read *The Way of the Prisoner*, and I autographed the book for him on the condition that he come back twice a month to help me form a meditation group. Without a clergy member to act as a monitor, we prisoners wouldn't be allowed to meet as a group, not even to meditate. We could be up to something.

Because Pastor Walter doesn't buy into the punishing God of "penal substitution," he now comes every second and fourth Saturday of the month to allow us dinosaurs to meditate together as a community instead of alone. Someone without any experience in meditation probably won't believe this, but something supernatural happens in that room. All of us feel it, and we've often spoken about it after a session. When you meditate as a community, the Way Inside opens up much more easily for everyone. This phenomenon is well known in Christian and Buddhist monasteries, but who would've guessed that it could also exist inside of a prison—amongst the "worst of the worst," no less?

Something else I share with Omo and L.A. is sports. Omo and I both love Tai Chi, and L.A. and I jog like lunatics. When it comes to Tai Chi and running, none of the younger guys can keep up with us old folk—we're still the champs!

Omo and L.A. are for me the black versions of my breakfast club partners Harry and Richard. They're a ray of hope, proof that all this pain and suffering can somehow be endured with dignity and honor. I don't need to brew a batch of "mash," enter into a prison "marriage," or cut my wrists. If these guys can make it without that kind of foolishness, I can, too. I *must* believe this, I *must* believe. . . .

At this hour, I can usually find Omo and L.A. at the infirmary because Omo has Hepatitis C, and L.A. often meets up with him to get a situation report. Hepatitis C is a disease of the liver that can go undetected for many years but almost always ends in death. Spread through sex, drug use with needles, and tattooing, this virus is much more easily transmitted than the HIV/AIDS virus, which is why 39 percent of all Virginia inmates have the disease.[61] That's approximately 13,650 people in Virginia alone.

The exact number of Hepatitis C carriers remains unknown, because almost all correctional facilities refuse to test all of their prisoners. The reason, according to *The New York Times* and the *Harper's* magazine, is the cost of treatment.[62] If you don't know exactly which inmates have Hepatitis C or HIV/AIDS, then you don't need to treat them. Another irony of corrections is that the money prison medical departments save must be spent later anyway—after the infected inmates are released and have transmitted their disease to their own friends and family members.[63]

No one has been courageous enough to tackle this problem up front, since the already existing health-care costs (i.e., without Hep C and HIV/AIDS prevention care) have exploded the budgets of correctional departments across the nation. In California, for example, so many prisoners died from fully preventable medical problems that in 2006 a judge took away control of the health-care system for inmates and placed it under the authority of a "special master," Robert Sillen. One of his interim reports stated that officials of the California Department of Corrections were actively attempting to obstruct his reform plan because, among other things, it was going to require an additional two *billion* dollars to provide the minimum standard of humane, professional, and, above all, constitutionally adequate medical care.[64] Those costs were *in addition to* the existing costs of correctional health services.

Experts agree that what California experienced is coming soon to a state near you. If Virginia, for instance, were to be forced by a special master to provide medical treatment to every person infected with Hepatitis C, costs would run from $202 million to $337 million per year![65] At present, the entire budget for the Virginia Department of Corrections is "only" one billion dollars annually.[66]

To avoid this financial calamity, prisoners are systematically discouraged from seeking medical treatment. Any inmate who requests a Hep C or HIV/AIDS test is provided one, free of charge; anything else would be inhumane! But in order to get the test, the prisoner must first secure an appointment with the physician, for which he is charged a $5 fee. For an inmate making the penitentiary minimum wage, five bucks is almost a quarter of his monthly pay. As a result, only a very few prisoners request tests, and most of these are careful about their health anyway. Which Porta-John™ prostitute is going to get tested when the news will almost certainly be bad for business?

If someone like Omo should get tested and seek treatment, correctional medical departments frequently impose conditions that must be fulfilled before the inmate receives his medication. It's a popular ploy: *You've got to go through substance-abuse counseling first, but unfortunately there aren't any openings at the moment. So sorry!*[67]

Because, as we've seen, the majority of inmates are either totally or functionally illiterate, they aren't able to overcome these bureaucratic hurdles. Omo is different in this respect: he's filed a legal complaint that he labored to prepare in the law library. Do-it-yourself lawsuits have only the slightest chance of success, since judges almost always find in favor of correctional medical departments.

If everyone delays enough, the irritating prisoner dies before too much money is wasted on treating him. *Harper's* managed to obtain internal documents from Correctional Medical Services that prove that this is indeed the intent: "protocol pathway" is the term used for this cost-effective but fatal delaying tactic.[68] In New York a government commission found that similar practices were employed by Prison Health Services, the company that manages our infirmary.[69] That's exactly what they're doing with Omo.

My friend is dying. His belly—that's to say his liver—is swollen, one of the symptoms of end-stage Hepatitis C. There's nothing that L.A. or I can do to help him. It's horrible to watch Omo die. Everything seems normal: the sun shines; the birds twitter; inmates pass us by, laughing. Even Omo smiles, blinks, and scratches at his gray beard—the beard, which is actually forbidden, like Ras Talawa Tafari's "dreadlocks," but which the authorities have let him keep because everybody knows he's going to die soon. What can L.A. and I say to him that will give him some comfort? Absolutely nothing.

We take leave of one another, feeling somehow awkward and embarrassed. Death and hopelessness drive us apart. I return to the honor building, where even more prisoners are sick with Hepatitis C. There's no help for them, either.

3:15 P.M.

As I enter my cell, it's almost count time and therefore I'm due for my third meditation period of the day, from twenty past three until four. Perhaps my conversation with Omo and L.A. has me thinking back to my youth and the double-murder for which I've been serving time since 1986. I don't think too much about these things any more.

During the first years I began meditating, all kinds of thoughts about that period of my life began to bubble up. It's normal and even necessary to work through your past once you enter the inner stillness; without this process of coming to terms with your life, you cannot go forward into the Eternal, the Good, and the True. For the majority of people—and certainly for me—the thickest bars and strongest walls of the prison of the "self" are the stories we tell ourselves about our past. We tend to see ourselves as innocent victims. How unfair it is that we've had to suffer through so much! How just and righteous we are in our feelings of anger at our persecutors! How noble we are that we've nevertheless forgiven the wretched dogs!

I lived and thought this way myself for many years. Like most people, I believed I had a particular right to see myself as a victim. After all, I'm serving time in prison for a crime I didn't commit.

I don't want to rehearse the 1985 crime yet again. It was written up in detail in the article "Trial and Error?" in the Charlottesville, Virginia, *Daily Progress* of January 21, 1996.

The author, Ian Zack, won an award for it in 1997, and it can be found on my website (www.jenssoering.com). The bottom line is that I am not a double-murderer. I *did* cover up the crime, which in Virginia is a misdemeanor not a felony.

For fourteen or fifteen years, from 1986 until I began meditating in 2000, I hung on to this fact for dear life. I saw myself as the innocent victim of a miscarriage of justice. I wanted nothing more than to prove this to the whole world in court. I also felt deep self-hatred, because it was through my own lies—the aforementioned cover-up—that I'd foolishly maneuvered myself into prison. The principal portion of the guilt, however, rested with the detective, the prosecutor, the judge, the witnesses, and my own incompetent lawyer. Self-pity was the essence of my life.

What surfaced repeatedly during my first year or two of meditation were deep feelings of guilt. Naturally, I refused to take these emotions seriously at first, since I was meant to be the victim! The wonderful thing about meditation is that you eventually stop fleeing and start seeing the bars and walls of the prison of the "self" for what they are. With time, my feelings of guilt crystallized around three specific events from the years 1985 and 1986. I'd recognized the importance of these incidents long before I began meditating, However, I'd always felt only profound self-hatred when I reflected on the grave mistakes I had made. Now I felt no self-hatred, but rather sadness and then an increasing sense of grief over what I'd brought about.

Looking back, I believe that this change took place because meditation allowed me to become aware of my own motivations. I'd always told myself that I'd covered up the crimes of my accomplice in order to save her from execution in the electric chair. This is true, but it's not the whole truth. Vanity and pride, fear and even desire also played an enormous, albeit subconscious role in my actions.

At the time I made those three crucial mistakes in 1985 and 1986, I'd not been aware of my own motivations for what I was doing. In the first decade and a half of my sentence I concentrated on the self-hatred I felt for allowing myself to be taken in by my accomplice and having thrown away my own life. Now I had to admit to myself that I was guilty. I may not have been guilty of the crime itself, but I was for the endless suffering I'd inflicted on so many people through my lies. In any case, I certainly am *not* without guilt.

That truth, which I gradually came to recognize and assimilate, wasn't depressing, but rather liberating. On some level, this is perhaps not so surprising: self-liberation—freedom from the "self"—is an important step on the long path into the inner realm, the Eternal, the Good, and the True. But how can something apparently negative, like the acceptance of guilt, lead to something positive, such as spiritual freedom?

When I stopped thinking of myself as a victim, I was finally able to stop hating myself for having allowed myself to *become* a victim. I've concluded that, generally speaking (not just in my case), self-hatred is an indicator of unconscious, repressed guilt that has yet to be acknowledged. Once you recognize the truth and take responsibility for that guilt, you no longer feel self-hatred but, instead, grief—the acceptance of loss. Out of that grief can emerge something constructive, like writing books, starting a meditation group, or leading a Tai Chi class. Self-hatred, on the other hand, robs you of the ability to do anything positive.

The recognition of my own guilt and responsibility also transformed my relationship with those I'd seen as my persecutors. The detective, prosecutor, judge, witnesses, my lawyer, and even my accomplice continue to bear responsibility for the fact that I'm still sitting in prison for something I didn't do. But instead of hating them all or "forgiving" them—begrudgingly and full of self-pity—I now see them all as my partners in crime. After all, who was the ringleader of the conspiracy that led to this miscarriage of justice? It was I.

My new understanding of my guilt also transformed my relationship with my fellow prisoners. From 1986 to 2000 I looked down on other inmates. All of them were more or less guilty, I decided; on the other hand, I was completely innocent. I distanced myself from them in small but deliberate ways simply to prove to myself how different I was. When the others, the guilty ones, watched a sports program on TV or read a western, I patted myself on my innocent back because I watched some political news show or read classics like Solzhenitsyn. How different, how much *better* I was in those years!

Today, that's over and done with. I consider myself to be just as guilty as Harry and Richard and Sylvester and Eugene and Liam and Willy and Omo and L.A., and all the others. Really, they're better than I am, since they never made the mistake of thinking themselves to be better.

Because of this, I feel myself more closely connected to these men than you, the reader of this book. For these men it's immaterial whether I committed a double-murder in 1985 or merely covered it up. For you and my friends in the outside world, the question of my guilt will always be an issue. This is not speculation. One of my unincarcerated friends deliberately avoids the subject and prefers not to discuss it at all; another is possessed with the thought of somehow proving my innocence. Yet a third reports to me that she heatedly debates the details of my case with a married couple who are friends of hers. Yet another says he believes I must be innocent because my books are so candid and honest.

I value the friendship of these wonderful people. In a certain respect they're right: it *does* matter whether I've been wrongly convicted, and whether the state of Virginia owes me a public apology, immediate release, and financial compensation. After all, we're *also* dealing with the objective integrity of the judicial system. Regardless of what they think, however, I know what I am and with whom I stand. I'm guilty, and I stand with the other guilty ones—my brothers and sisters in chains.

4:00 P.M.

At four, the cell doors are unlocked once again and it's time for dinner. The honor building is the first housing unit to be called to the dining hall today, so we all run directly from our cells to the sliding double doors at the entryway. Next to the control room is a bit of a traffic jam: during count time an announcement from the prison administration has been taped to the wall, and it's causing quite a stir.

The Discovery Channel is back on! In the penitentiary, this channel is extremely popular because it airs programs on motorcycle repair, nature and wildlife, and many other subjects the inmates' hearts yearn after. For about two weeks, the Discovery Channel has been switched off; nobody seems to know why. The assistant warden received an avalanche of complaints about it—her desk almost sags from the mountains of paperwork. Now we are promised that everything is back to normal: the infamous "technical problems" have been fixed.

Because I watch only the news on TV, my sympathy for my fellow prisoners is somewhat limited. Quite apart from this, I wonder if there's nothing better for us to complain about than the loss of one of the TV channels. Is that really the most important issue we have to protest against? But it's always the small, insignificant things that cause the most complaints. A few months ago, it was the selection of ice cream flavors. I feel like pulling my hair out and asking myself: *Who is really crazy here? The inmates who man the barricades only when it's about the*

TV or ice cream? Or I, who begrudges them the fact they want to hold on to their few small pleasures?

From the perspective of the prison administration, it's extremely helpful that the mental horizon of the inmate population is so restricted. I don't know whether the "technical problems" with the Discovery Channel were genuine or if they were intentionally engineered. But there's no doubt that in general prisoners are regularly manipulated through the creation of minor problems. These divert our attention from larger issues and we're always grateful to the administration when they solve one of them.

In a police interrogation, this strategy is called "good cop/bad cop." One of the officers threatens you while the other is understanding and friendly. In this situation, too, one tends to concentrate on the small problem at hand, such as how one can get a cigarette. The good cop has one ready, and you feel so much gratitude that you roll over and confess.

Having gone through that process at the time of our arrest, you'd think we inmates would be aware of this ploy. Nevertheless, we fall for it time and again, even after decades behind bars. The need for love is deeply rooted in the heart of every person. Even we villains need to believe that someone wants to do something nice for us—that someone really cares. The cigarette during interrogation and the Discovery Channel in the penitentiary are signs of love! And because there's so little love in our lives, it's ridiculously easy to manipulate us through our hearts.

Such is the case today. Many men on their way to the dining hall should have been released years ago. Many have medical problems like Hepatitis C or heart disease that haven't been properly treated. Many will die in prison. But all of that's forgotten, because the Discovery Channel is back on. *Aren't we incredibly lucky to live in such a wonderful penitentiary, where the administration takes such good care of us?*

In the dining hall I take one of the 61-cent trays from the hole in the wall and sit with a couple of guys to make our previously arranged food trades. I give the dry, stale cookies to one, and hand over the sawdust-and-soy sausage to the other. From both, I get peas—*real* peas—in return. We haven't seen peas for more than a year.

Following our housing unit, the next building to be called to the dining hall is the Mental Health Unit, so we're able to watch the mentally ill stand in line while we eat. This is commonplace for us, but for those of you who haven't experienced it the scene before us must be unimaginable—something out of eighteenth-century Bedlam. That something like this still exists in this country. . . .

The first thing you notice about these prisoners is their slow, foot-dragging gait, the stiff movements and the slouched posture. The men's stares seem directed at something far, far away. Their mouths are often half-open, with dried spittle in the corners. You can see and smell that they're dirty—their hair, face, and especially their hands. Their clothing is covered in cigarette ashes, bits of food, and just plain filth. Many are not only mentally ill but also developmentally disabled, as one can see from their facial features and expressions and even damaged skulls. Some exhibit stereotypical grimaces or simply laugh out loud.

I've maintained a funny kind of friendship for several years with one of these men. Arthur is a tall, slender black man who combs his gray hair straight up and is constantly chewing on his lower lip. Every time he sees me he yells, "Hello there, Star Trek!" It was several years before I finally asked him why he always greeted me that way. "Because you remind me of one of the actors on *Star Trek*," Arthur told me. So I answered him with the words, "Beam me up." We always greet each other in this fashion now, something that Arthur finds extremely funny. Yesterday, he came to Mass for the first time. "God bless you, Star Trek," he said to me.

So it goes with the poor souls who live on the first and second floor of the Mental Health Unit. Those who live on the third floor also show physical signs of mental challenges, but their symptoms are perhaps less severe. Their movements are more certain, they don't appear to be quite as unfocused, and most of them are more hygienic. But when you take a few minutes to speak with them, you notice very quickly that they, too, are severely damaged. One man—a small, skinny white guy named Zach—is so incredibly plagued with fear that he hardly ever dares to leave his housing unit. When you try to put yourself in his shoes, you can't help but admire Zach as the bravest person in the penitentiary. What internal obstacles he must have to overcome simply to get to the dining hall!

I observe these people in the line for their dinner as I eat my own. Once they've got their trays, they spread out among the tables and try to find someone who will trade them a few cigarettes for some portion of their tray, or even the entire meal itself. This is a rule violation, so these transactions must take place covertly.

The guards cannot stop this food bartering completely since the majority of Mental Health Unit residents are fiercely addicted to nicotine. All day long, they scour the compound for thrown-away butts and argue among themselves about who gets to claim the especially rich pickings from the trash can next to the dining-hall door. Some will do anything for a bit of tobacco, including giving oral sex in the Porta-John™ on the rec yard. Others have learned that they can sell their psychotropic medication if they spit it back out after visiting the infirmary's pill window. With that kind of business acumen, it's a wonder that Keefe and MCI WorldCom haven't hired our mentally ill inmates.

If they're caught, these men will be locked up in punitive seg., which is located in the basement of the honor building. As I write, such a man is sitting in the cell directly below mine.

He's quiet at the moment, but last night he was howling a wordless and uninterrupted *Wooooooooh!* He's probably afraid of retaliation from the inmate he snitched on. The mentally ill prisoner had borrowed some cigarettes and gave the loan shark his necklace and cross as collateral. Because he later regretted the deal, the prisoner asked a guard for help: he wanted his Jesus back. The guard threw both of them in the hole, since both had committed a violation of Rule 227: "Unauthorized transfer of personal property." In one case it was the cigarettes; in the other it was the necklace and cross.

In a couple of days, both men will be released from punitive seg., and then comes the reckoning. *Wooooooh!* For all that, this poor guy still has it relatively good, since the majority of correctional facilities have no special psychiatric units like those at Brunswick's. Everywhere else, people like Arthur and Zach and the nameless howler in the basement are simply thrown into the regular housing units—food for the sharks.

Approximately one-fifth of all prison inmates have been officially diagnosed and classified as mentally ill[70]—a fraction that amounts to more than 400,000 men, women, and juveniles who obviously belong in psychiatric clinics rather than penitentiaries. In the seventies and eighties, most of those facilities closed down. It was believed that these people could be better treated on an outpatient basis. However, the community treatment programs designed to fulfill this purpose were never implemented.[71]

Recent estimates by mental health–care professionals suggest that there should be approximately 930,000 patients in psychiatric facilities. In actuality, there are only 60,000: the remainder are in prison or jail, or out on bail or probation.[72] The two largest mental health-services providers in the nation are not a hospital or clinic, but rather the Los Angeles and New York City jails. In these prisons the mentally ill are invisible—hidden away better than they ever were in the old-style hospitals or clinics. No one needs to care for them anymore, because they're officially labeled "criminals." They're no longer *sick*, but *bad*. At last, they can be punished: hard but fair.

Zach, my fearful acquaintance from the Mental Health Unit, probably grasps the reality of the situation more precisely and clearly than the rest of us. What's been done to these hundreds of thousands of people should make us all afraid. In the past, before America went prison-crazy, a wonderful, old-fashioned word for the suffering inflicted on the mentally ill existed: *satanic*.

4:55 P.M.

Upon my return to the honor building, I run into Bud, who's flipping out again in the dayroom. For some obscure reason, the starting time for the Alcoholics Anonymous group has been postponed; such things are constantly happening in the penitentiary. For Bud, though, this self-help group for alcoholics is a kind of substitute religion, so he always becomes extremely agitated when such problems occur.

As with Harry and Richard, my breakfast-club partners, Bud is a veteran of the Vietnam conflict. He took a little longer than they to get to the point where the psychological damage from the war and the drinking caused an explosion. Now he's serving 127 years. The only thing that makes his life worth living is the belief that he can help save other prisoners from a similar fate through his efforts in the A.A. group.

Bud is a fanatic: in some ways admirable, but nevertheless more than a little high strung. Today, he's not actually ranting over the delay but is instead snorting and growling and stomping back and forth between the control room and his cell. Every resident of the honor building knows to avoid any contact with him at times like this. What he's looking for is someone who will listen to him. When that someone has been caught, he gets the full force of Bud's standard tirade: how much better he could run things, how much nicer everything used to be, how much all of this reminds him of Vietnam. Then comes the story about the helicopter being shot down and the captivity as a POW. All of that happened in the early seventies, and he still suffers from it to this day.

In one respect, Bud's outrage over the delay of the A.A. group is fully justified; it's the sole source of hope for the many inmates addicted to alcohol. Thirty-seven percent of prisoners were under the influence of alcohol at the time of their crimes, and 33 percent were under the influence of drugs.[73] Everyone knows that the recidivism rates of substance abusers can be reduced from 75 percent to 27 percent through real treatment programs.[74] But only 5 percent of the annual corrections budget of $63 billion is devoted to therapeutic and educational programs.[75] Even the model prison of Brunswick has no single official program for alcoholics. Only Bud—the worst of the worst—cares enough to organize the weekly A.A. group for the seven to ten inmates who depend on the meetings.

Today, Bud—or rather the potential target of his angry tirade—is in luck: Mrs. Jefferson walks into the dayroom and tells us that all prisoners participating in programs this evening can now leave the building. Bud is happy, as am I, because I can now go to the gym to lead my Tai Chi class. This is the second, much less filthy part to my job in the gym.

I pass by the Watch Office where close to a dozen inmates are waiting for their substance abuse class to begin. Twelve men constitutes less than 2 percent of Brunswick's incarcerated population, even though 76.2 percent of all prisoners have either drug or alcohol problems.[76] These twelve aren't receiving any real therapy, but a class led by a correctional caseworker. His job consists primarily of evaluating the security levels of the inmates on his caseload. If one has too many points—perhaps because of a rule violation, let's say—the caseworker submits the paperwork to have that prisoner transferred to a higher-security level prison.

Obviously, this makes it impossible for prisoners to confide in this man. Anything we say can and will be used against us.

The caseworker leading the substance-abuse class this evening hasn't received any specialized education in drug therapy or rehab. Is it any wonder that I don't see any great hope in the faces of the inmates waiting for the class to begin? They're in that room only because their own caseworkers have ordered them to be there.

After I step through the gate to the rec yard, I turn right and follow the outer wall of the gym to the entrance. In the middle of this long wall is the window where we can exchange for pints of ice cream the little blue tickets purchased in the Keefe store. The window is open at the moment, and today the line is particularly long because the sawdust-and-soy sausage we had for dinner was especially inedible.

Can it really be a coincidence that the prison kitchen is serving more unpalatable food—and less of it—precisely at the time when corrections officials are inventing ever more ways for us to buy ice cream and food packages and other such food-stuffs? Or is my suspicion just a paranoid delusion, or even a particularly elaborate distortion of the truth? Who knows? My penitentiary file states that I'm a sociopathic manipula-tive genius, so I'm not to be trusted. On the other hand, if the bureaucrats at the correctional headquarters in Richmond actually *are* manipulating our hunger to acquire our money, then *they* would be the sociopaths. Let's not think too much about that frightening possibility.

Among those in the ice-cream line this evening are four of the juveniles housed at Brunswick. Approximately 11,000 boys and girls who were minors at the time of their offenses must, like these young men, serve their sentences in an adult facil-ity.[77] Before their trials, these juveniles were legally certified as adults under the principle that if they were old enough to do the crime, they were old enough to do the time.

How insane this practice is evident when one looks at these four children. Some seventeen-year-olds appear almost adult, but each one of this quartet is so small and slight that they barely reach my shoulder. None of them has even the least bit of fuzz on their upper lip; on closer examination, I can detect a couple of frizzy hairs on the cheek of one of the boys. He's probably proud of it and thinks it makes him a man.

What is touching about these four midgets is that they aren't even trying to give the impression of being the rebellious hard-asses they're supposed to be. Instead, they huddle together and keep their eyes glued to the ground so as to avoid any accidental eye contact with us grown-ups. Was I that shy and fearful when I came to prison in 1986? I was perhaps one or two years older, although I was certainly more inexperienced than these four. But I don't believe I was as intimidated as these kids seem to be. What's been said or done to them to make them like this?

In the majority of correctional facilities children are mixed in with the adult population and even placed in double cells with grown-ups. As a result, youths housed in adult facilities are five times more likely to be violently assaulted and eight times more likely to commit suicide than those housed in juvenile facilities.[78] Fortunately, the model prison of Brunswick is different. Minors are placed on one hall and housed in a double cell only with other juveniles. All adults on that hall are warned not to lay a hand on the lads or face a potential charge of child molestation.

Even though the minors were certified as adults so they could be prosecuted and sent to an adult penitentiary, they are legally considered children once they arrive here. If, for example, a convict were to give a pack of cigarettes or a *Playboy* magazine to a juvenile, he could be prosecuted for "contributing to the delinquency of a minor." If one of the boys skips school, he can be charged with truancy—a misdemeanor under Virginia law.

As usual, I'm amused at the swirl of emotions that seize me

on such occasions. I feel pain when I encounter this kind of helplessness, no doubt because it mirrors my own. I become angry at all those who are responsible for such conditions and refuse to consider the suffering of these children. I'm then overtaken by a desire for revenge: *I'll put this little scene into my next book,* that's *what I'll do. Then those awful people will finally feel some real regret when they read what their heartlessness has brought about.* At that point, I have to laugh at myself and my delusions of literary grandeur. What politician or corrections official is going to read my books? Finally, I feel a kind of gratitude that after more than two decades behind bars I'm still not so hardened that I don't become outraged when I see injustice and inhumanity.

With a little smile, I pass by the four boys and step into the gym, where the twelve members of my Tai Chi class are waiting for me. All kinds of strange birds have joined this group—folks who, like me, simply don't fit in prison: two child molesters, two effeminate homosexuals, two guys from the Mental Health Unit, two of the extreme loners found everywhere in the penitentiary, two shell-shocked members of the middle class, and even two jocks who have too much gray matter to lift weights and play softball *all* the time. As with the animals in Noah's ark, they seem to come in pairs. Somehow we try to weather the storm of prison life together—for an hour, anyway.

Tai Chi is a Chinese exercise that looks like Kung Fu in slow motion. It's proven to benefit those with high blood pressure and arthritis, reduce stress, and even has a spiritual side to it as a form of "moving meditation." Because it is performed very slowly, with great deliberation, Tai Chi forces you to focus only on the present moment, instead of mourning the past or anxiously anticipating the future. It's unbelievably relaxing— and real, deep relaxation is a true luxury in the penitentiary.

Perhaps the most interesting facet of Tai Chi is that it can be practiced in a group. Since all participants are performing exactly the same movements simultaneously, you feel that you belong to a flock of birds soaring through the air. For a little while, at least, you can overcome that great bane of prison life, the feeling that you're completely alone. In the Tai Chi group, for a little while, we are one.

Tai Chi also promotes a certain elegance and grace, a gentleness and beauty in the manner in which one performs the movements. The penitentiary has very few traces of elegance and grace, so it's always a shock to chance upon a Tai Chi group in motion. When else does an inmate have the opportunity to experience himself as gentle or beautiful?

If you think about it, Tai Chi shouldn't be allowed to exist in a correctional facility. Our little group is the total antithesis of punishment, and it's not even a typical rehabilitation program because it doesn't therapeutically address any specific "problem." The class ought to be forbidden. Perhaps after the publication of this book it will be.

6:30 P.M.

At half past six it's gate break: the Tai Chi class ends, and we strange birds part ways and fly back to our respective housing units. I'm feeling a little tired, since my day began at twenty past four in the morning. The other prisoners on the rec yard are all quite active as I cross it to reach the gate.

A game is underway on the softball field, and several dozen inmates are either walking or jogging on the track that encircles it. Another group is doing pull-ups and push-ups, while the picnic tables are being utilized for high-stakes card games. On the paved sidewalk next to the Keefe store, the Dungeons & Dragons® players have spread out some towels so they can battle each other as knights, wizards, or hobbits for a couple of hours.

Further along the same sidewalk some Muslim prisoners are kneeling to perform their evening prayers. On the other side of the fence separating the visiting room from the rec yard, the Protestants are holding their service as well. The door to the visiting room has been left half open because of the heat, so you can hear the rhythmic hand-clapping and soulful cadences of the gospel choir. Unfortunately, the barbed wire fence isn't the only thing that separates these two groups. Although the conflict is not as bad at Brunswick as in other penitentiaries, even here religious groups sometimes function as quasi–prison gangs. We tend to segregate ourselves in all sorts of ways, especially by skin color.

Leaving the rec yard I again pass by the infirmary on my

way back to the honor building, where I take my second shower of the day—another luxury. While drying off in my cell, I switch on my five-inch-screen TV to watch the News Hour on PBS. The arrest of the "Monster of the Week" that was covered so sensationally on the morning news isn't mentioned on this newscast this evening. This is the real news, not the stuff of the tabloids.

After a few minutes I switch off the TV and head into the dayroom because my cellmate wants to use the toilet before we're locked in for the next count time. As always at this time of day, the dayroom is noisy. A card game is in progress, and the big TV is tuned to a baseball game. At least it's not on BET®, and for that bit of mercy I'm truly thankful.

I stand to the side. These men are my brothers, to be sure, but I don't fit into any of their groups. Many of the honor-building residents don't trust me fully since my life is so evidently different from theirs. For most of them, the word "book" refers to a porn magazine, not a literary project. And the constant meditation—*what's that nonsense about?*

I'd like to be able to report that a fellow inmate brought my loneliness to an end in some touching, perhaps even edifying, manner. Who doesn't love a happy ending? But nobody has come, and I haven't found anybody. In the penitentiary you're never alone, but you're forever lonely.

After a few minutes, I return to the cell because the guard is in the process of passing out the mail. I receive several letters almost every evening, and in that respect I'm much better off than the majority of prisoners. In some ways, however, mail from the outside world actually heightens my loneliness. Each letter reminds me of the life on the outside I could have had. I cannot help but remember that, unlike free-worlders, I'm *not* able simply to go to dinner or a concert with these friends.

My correspondents constantly, if inadvertently, remind me of all the things I don't have in prison: children, for instance.

I often hear from my friends about their kids, and I would've liked to have had children of my own very much. Each letter brings home to me once again how little my friends really understand my world and my problems. We truly live on completely different planets.

Most significantly perhaps, the letters are only paper. One of the strangest aspects of this life behind bars is that inmates almost never touch one another, with only two exceptions: homosexual contact and the embrace during church services. For mammals like us *Homo sapiens*, physical contact with fellow members of the same species is an absolute necessity. My own opinion is that the absence of normal physical touching is one of the primary causes of the deep psychological damage brought about by incarceration. Letters don't help in this respect at all.

Luckily, some of my friends don't limit themselves to letters, but also come to visit me. A few years ago, for instance, an especially attractive young woman who'd fallen in love with my books came to see me. During the entire two or three hours of the visit we held hands—as is allowed. At the end, following the rules exactly, we kissed once—perhaps somewhat longer than is allowed. It was my first kiss in almost twenty years and was simultaneously unbelievably wonderful and painful. I had totally forgotten that something as soft as these lips existed.

After the kiss I returned to the housing unit. My cellmate at the time was using the bathroom, so that place of refuge was denied me. Experienced jailbird that I am, I went straight to the broom closet diagonally across from my cell, pulled the door closed behind me, and cried like a baby. During the few seconds of that kiss, I was a human being, a real, true person. I wasn't a subhuman, or a prisoner, but Jens Soering. Now I was once again 179212.

Since then I've had to live with the memory of that kiss and my temporary personhood. I've had to deal with the overwhelming probability that I'll never again be allowed to be a human being. For me, there's no longer any hope in this world.

But can you really live without any hope at all?

This is the second time in my life I've had to seriously consider this question. The first occasion was when I was arrested on April 30, 1986, while on the run in London, England. When the prosecuting attorney from Virginia submitted an extradition request to the British government, he made it known that he would do everything in his power to ensure my execution. My own lawyers told me that there was no hope. "You're going to die in the electric chair," they said.

My attorneys submitted an appeal against the extradition request. They told me that I had no chance of success, but it would prolong my life a bit. Approximately every six months the attorneys would send me copies of their appellate briefs, which described in full detail the process of execution in the electric chair. They wanted to use these gruesome accounts to convince the European Court of Human Rights to deny my extradition to the U.S.

I spent the years 1986 to 1989 reading over and over again about the smell of burning human flesh ("like fried pork") and burning hair, of eyeballs popping out of their sockets, of the four or five electroshocks that had to be applied within a fifteen-minute period because the criminal simply refused to die. I dealt with the stress by eating an ungodly amount of Twix® candy bars, and by keeping a rope I'd made from torn bed sheets hidden in my cell. I planned to hang myself as soon as the last appeal against my extradition had been denied.

In this way, my sole purpose in life consisted of denying the Virginians the pleasure of executing me—by killing myself just in time. I lived for death.

Astonishingly enough, the European Court of Human Rights decided in 1989 to deny my extradition to Virginia as long as the death penalty hung over my head. A huge victory, we all thought. . . . So in 1990, after the prosecutor withdrew the capital murder indictment, I was sent to Virginia and shortly afterward sentenced to two life terms. At that time, this sentence meant that I could expect to be deported to Germany in fifteen to seventeen years. But in 1995 Virginia abolished early release on parole, and so any real possibility of deportation to Germany was *de facto* abolished as well.

As in England from 1986 to 1989, I now once again have no reason to hope. A life sentence for me and the 130,000 other lifers in this country is a kind of death penalty: execution on the installment plan. True, we're not sitting in the electric chair, but the authorities are executing us nevertheless—just more slowly.

This existence—I don't want to call it a life—turns out to be harder to bear than those nightmarish years in England. In the 1980s there was at least the certainty of a coming deliverance: death, whether by the electric chair or suicide. A person can stand almost any amount of suffering as long as he knows there's an end in sight. What I have now is the certainty that my execution is going to last my entire lifetime.

This life is bearable for me only through meditation. I tried meditation in England, but I simply didn't succeed. Since 2001, however, it's been different, and now everything has changed. I no longer hide a homemade rope in my cell, and candy bars (Twix or otherwise) are a once-monthly treat.

What meditation has given me is not something I can describe as *hope* or *faith* but perhaps *knowledge* and *understanding*. Only a half hour before I wrote these lines, I was once again in that clear, open space where, if I remain perfectly still, I encounter the Eternal, the Good, and the True. I don't need faith for this: I *know* without a doubt that this trinity existed before the world came to be, and that I'll exist within it long after the world has passed. This world, this time, these life sentences, the books that must be written, those lips that I'll never again kiss—all will pass and melt away, like a mist.

Through this knowledge, through this direct contact with this Truth in meditation—through this can I yet live, this one day in the life of 179212.

At a quarter before eight the doors are locked shut because it's count time once again. For the next ten or fifteen minutes I read an English translation of Meister Eckhart, a German mystic of the fourteenth century. "God is a pure no-thing, he is not touched by any now or here." Right you are, Meister Eckhart, right you are! Meister Eckhart was a Dominican, a so-called "dog of God" (Latin: *domini canis*). In this way, I too am able to participate in the Pen Pals program: my dog's name is Eckhart!

I'm not allowed to read Meister Eckhart's works in German, because it might contain subversive information about escape. Ironically, Meister Eckhart's words free me from prison even through the English translation. If the corrections officials only knew. . . .

At five minutes before eight two guards blow into their whistles and peer into each cell door window. As soon as they've gone by, I brush my teeth, pee, turn off the light, and climb into the top bunk. My cellmate watches TV for another half hour or so, and then he too lies down to sleep.

As I do every night, I try to find words to pray, something I find increasingly more difficult: God and I understand each other better without words. But I won't begrudge Him an Our Father and a Nicene Creed! I pray for my friends in the outside world and my friends in prison. Finally, I pray the last verse of Psalm 142:

Lead us out of our prison
> that we may give thanks to your name.
Then the just will gather around us
> because you have been good to us.

In the original this Psalm is in the singular ("Lead me . . . ," etc.), but I pray it in the plural ("Lead us . . . ") because, in my humble opinion, it wouldn't hurt God one little bit to release not only me, but all of the other prisoners in this book.

Then I say, "Amen," turn over, and immediately fall off to sleep.

Afterword

THE STORY OF JENS SOERING

Patricia McGinty

Jens Soering opens his eyes every morning—and he's still in prison, and still in the U.S. The memories are still there, too.

The bars on the window, the cramped cell, the narrow bed, the ugly gray walls, the iron grate on the door, the noise in front of the cell all remind him of his first love and his greatest mistake.

He's in prison for life for a love that hasn't survived.

He cannot escape from the memory. He cannot run away from it no matter how fast he jogs on the prison yard. He cannot shake it off, cannot hide from it, and will never be rid of it. It is always with him, loyal, pale, and insistent: the memory of his youthful love.

Jens Soering met Elizabeth Haysom in the fall of 1984 at the University of Virginia. Both of them were in their first semester. Jens was 18 years old, and Elizabeth 20. She was attractive, capricious, and eccentric. He was a young, inexperienced, awkward over-achiever.

Elizabeth was a charismatic personality—interesting, intelligent, entertaining—who possessed a vivid imagination and a loose relationship with the truth. She loved to provoke and to cause turmoil. A Canadian with a distinguished British boarding-school accent, she was a gifted storyteller with a penchant for exaggeration and embellishment. She cast a spell over her fellow students with her colorful tales of a wild past, bisexual experiences, and journeys through Europe. Unusual, unconventional, unpredictable, rebellious—that was Elizabeth!

She hated to be told what to do, refused to conform to social conventions, and boastfully told stories of drug use, sexual abuse, and rape. She liked to shock her audience and reveled in their dismay and embarrassment.

Jens was captivated. For him, Elizabeth was an introduction to an undreamed-of new world. He'd had a sheltered and privileged childhood, protected by private schools from the outside world. Nothing in his past had prepared him for this new world of drugs, crime, abuse, violence, and mental illness.

Jens was fascinated by Elizabeth, with her unusual life, her talent, her vibrant account of an adventurous past. What he admired most was that she'd retained her vivacity despite terrible circumstances and dreadful misfortunes. Jens lacked any life-experience that might have enabled him to recognize neurotic or psychotic traits in her behavior and tall tales.

As a would-be author and artist, Elizabeth felt that she needed to defy her parents and the life they'd planned for her in order to develop her own unique genius. She was strangely persuasive and convincing, weaving a mysterious magic when she spoke; her listeners hung on her every word.

Jens was not the only one mesmerized by Elizabeth. A professor described her as the "queen bee of the university." Half of her student dorm, boys and girls, were hopelessly in love with her.

When, of all people, she chose the know-it-all German to be her lover in December of 1984, the campus erupted in indignation and outrage. They were such an unlikely couple! Jens was unbelievably proud and astonished that Elizabeth would pick him from among all her other suitors. It was Jens' first adult relationship, and he was in every respect immature, inexperienced, and innocent. Many students continued to desire Elizabeth and worship her from afar, and they were all jealous of Jens, furious that he'd taken her from them.

Jens Soering was born in Bangkok, Thailand, in 1966. His family was from Germany, his father a diplomat, and the Soerings moved frequently to follow Jens' father to new postings. Jens spent the first years of his life with his parents on the island of Cyprus where his younger brother was born, followed by a couple of uneventful years in Germany. Then, when Jens was eleven years old, the family moved to the United States, where his father had taken an assignment working for the German consulate general in Atlanta, Georgia. Summer vacations, however, were always spent in Germany or Switzerland.

The family placed a great deal of importance on education and refined manners, and Jens and his brother attended one of Atlanta's finest private schools. Having understood early on that his mother had a problem with alcohol, Jens made it his habit to protect her and went to great lengths to stand out from the crowd through especially good behavior and outstanding academic achievement. Jens spent as much time as possible at school and involved himself in countless extracurricular activities and clubs. Even though English was not his native language and the family spoke only German at home, he was at the top of his class in English and became editor of the school paper.

Germany remained home for Jens. In America, he always felt unsure of himself—an outsider who never quite fit in. Perhaps because he excelled only in academics but not athletics, American girls weren't necessarily fond of him. His German background turned out to be something of a hindrance: he struggled with a poor self-image and self-doubt. No one noticed that his social development lagged far behind his intellectual capability, a fact obscured by his phenomenal academic achievements.

Jens dreamed of one day returning to Germany to attend university and complete his studies there. Then, in 1984, Jens became the recipient of a coveted academic scholarship to the University of Virginia. His parents were understandably excited and proud, but Jens was secretly disappointed. Now his return to Germany would be delayed indefinitely.

At the University of Virginia, however, he found himself surrounded for the first time in his life by like-minded individuals, high-flyers, geniuses, and scholarship students. He finally felt like he belonged.

Elizabeth was Jens' first serious girlfriend, his first experience with love. They were inseparable, wrote long, brooding letters to each other, and stayed up all night discussing philosophy and literature. As a way of demonstrating her love for him—so she said—Elizabeth gave up drugs. Jens gave her strength; she needed only his love in her life. He was only too ready and willing to believe her.

Not long after the beginning of their relationship, Elizabeth took Jens to her parents' house while they weren't home. She was quiet and unresponsive as she showed him nude photographs that her mother had taken of her. Having shown Jens the drawer where the pictures were kept, and the stack of photos itself, she refused to discuss the matter further. Jens had no notion of how to cope with the situation and reacted awkwardly and ineptly.

The Haysoms were a well-respected family in Lynchburg, Virginia. Elizabeth's mother, Nancy Astor Haysom, came from an aristocratic family that moved in the best circles, were regarded as witty, and enjoyed popularity and high social standing.

Elizabeth was the youngest and only child of her parents, though both Haysoms had children from previous marriages. Including Elizabeth, there were six children altogether. The age difference between Elizabeth and her half-siblings was so great, however, that she virtually grew up as an only child. Because she was gifted, her parents sent her to the best schools.

Elizabeth found the expensive and elite boarding schools in Switzerland and England to be hostile and smothering environments. Throughout her youth she resisted the influence and control of her parents through rebellion. She smoked cigarettes, abused drugs, and ran away from school. The last time she absconded, she and a friend tramped through Europe for a year, financing their day-to-day needs and heroin habits however they could. Eventually, the two were discovered, and Elizabeth was sent back to the U.S.

Her parents tried desperately to get Elizabeth to see reason, and she finally agreed to a compromise. In August of 1984 she enrolled at the University of Virginia in nearby Charlottesville.

Jens met the Haysoms in February 1985 at a luncheon date with Elizabeth on the campus of the university. They spent a little more than half an hour making polite conversation. According to Jens, this was the first and only time he encountered the Haysoms.

That April, Elizabeth Haysom's parents were found dead in their home. The scene was grizzly: they had been stabbed to death, suffering numerous knife wounds after trying to flee in two different directions. Nancy was 53 and her husband Derek was 72.

What exactly took place depends upon who is telling the story. Jens' account has remained unchanged since 1990.

On March 30, 1985, Jens and Elizabeth made plans for a romantic weekend in Washington, D.C., reserving a rental car and a room at the Marriott hotel. But on Saturday afternoon at lunch Elizabeth unexpectedly cut the weekend short: she had to quickly drive back to Charlottesville to do a favor for her drug dealer in order to settle a debt. Jens was less than enthusiastic over this revelation and abrupt change in plans, but he offered to go with her to protect her. Elizabeth brushed aside this suggestion. Jens wasn't exactly suitable protection for this kind of situation, since he was too clean-cut and would arouse the dealer's suspicion. Instead, she said, he should remain in D.C. and purchase two tickets for different movies in order to provide her with an alibi in case her parents became suspicious and began asking questions.

Elizabeth's parents knew nothing of the secret lovers' weekend in D.C., nor of the heroin addiction. The drug dealer, who happened to be a scholarship student at the University of Virginia, was also the son of acquaintances of the Haysoms, and it was possible they might discover something through him. Elizabeth, seemingly remorseful, promised Jens that after this weekend she would once and for all get her addiction under control. As happened so often, Jens accepted her promise.

Jens stayed behind in D.C., unhappy and uneasy, resentfully going to three different movies and then returning to the hotel to wait far into the night for Elizabeth, full of concern. Elizabeth arrived back at the hotel room in the early hours of the morning, pale, distraught, agitated, and wearing different clothes from those she had worn the day before. She seemed completely shook up, repeating over and over again, "I've killed my parents, I've killed my parents."

Her greatest concern was the death penalty—that she would end up dying in the electric chair. Jens was horrified. The Haysoms, the crime scene, the crime itself—he dared not think of any of these things. His only thought was for Elizabeth, who was in mortal danger.

So Jens leapt into action as the hero to save the day. With his own characteristic perfectionism, he chose a solution to the problem that wasn't just good enough, but exceptionally, unusually, phenomenally, outstandingly good. Mediocrity was never his thing! Such an extraordinary problem demanded an extraordinary solution.

Jens was pressed for time—surely the police were hot on Elizabeth's heels. Because he hadn't done anything to prevent the tragedy, he felt partially responsible for it; and because he'd prepared an alibi for Elizabeth, he felt partially guilty. He was scared for Elizabeth; he couldn't allow her to be taken from him; he had to come up with a plan! Fully in the grip of this over-zealousness and catastrophic youthful over-confidence, Jens made the greatest—and, surprisingly enough, the dumbest—mistake of his life. In stark contrast to the normal operation of his sharp mind and intelligence, these extreme conditions revealed in him a tragic lack of life-experience, realistic self-awareness, and self-esteem.

Jens offered to take the blame for Elizabeth.

It was an utterly foolish idea, the high point of confusion, youthful hubris, self-sacrifice, and destructive love. It was a misunderstanding of love and altruism—an entire century's worth of misinterpreted romantic literature. The hero would sacrifice himself and save the life of his love, as did Sydney Carton in Charles Dickens' *A Tale of Two Cities*.

A call to the police, a doctor, to Jens' parents or some other adult, and Jens might today have a relatively normal life. It's easy to say in retrospect. Jens knows this only too well.

Jens is tortured day after day by this mistake. He agonizes about every detail of that night, asking himself how his life might have turned out if only he'd done something differently. He lives with the consequences of his own stupidity, and because of it he's developed a deep self-hatred. He sees only too clearly that he failed in that moment—he, who'd never before failed in his life. He'd always been successful; everything came so easily and effortlessly to him. For him, no problem didn't have a solution.

Jens assumed that his father's diplomatic status would extend to him in the form of immunity from prosecution, that on the basis of his German citizenship his case would be tried in a German court and he would be sentenced in the German juvenile justice system.

All these assumptions would later prove to be false.

Jens and Elizabeth spent the rest of the night constructing a plan, getting their stories straight, and preparing for interrogation by the police. In their desperation they reached for something familiar, from the intellectual domain of their university studies. They based their plan on Shakespeare's *Macbeth*. Later at his trial, Jens was dismayed that no one at those crass proceedings appreciated this fine literary nuance.

After this night, Jens and Elizabeth would never again speak of the crime or of what happened.

At the funeral for her parents, Elizabeth appeared quiet and composed, but her brothers and sisters were in absolute turmoil. The whole neighborhood was traumatized; this was the most grizzly crime that Bedford County had ever seen. Jens was bordering on hysteria from nervousness and panic, and was in real danger of cracking under the strain of keeping the secret. When confronted with the grief of the older Haysom siblings, he almost lost his composure and nearly betrayed everything.

Jens gave serious consideration to killing himself and leaving behind a letter in which he would assume all guilt and absolve

Elizabeth of all blame, thereby fulfilling his promise to her. Elizabeth, however, pressed him to hold fast to their original plan, and in a long letter she reminded Jens of their agreement.

After the funeral, the two returned to college in order to maintain the appearance of normality. The secrecy welded the two even closer together; the relationship between Jens and Elizabeth became symbiotic, monopolizing, consuming, and destructive. Speaking to no one of their anguish, the couple drew further and further away from other people and existed only with and for each other—two against the rest of the world. This transformation would later be diagnosed by psychiatrists as "folie à deux," a "madness for two" or shared psychotic disorder. Jens consoled himself with the thought that Elizabeth's act was self-defense. He didn't ask what happened that night. He didn't want to know. Even though the terrible secret of the crime formed the center of their lives, the crime and sequence of events were never discussed for an entire year. They referred to it only as "our little nasty."

The law enforcement authorities in Virginia were under enormous pressure to solve the Haysom case; only when the perpetrator was brought to justice could the neighborhood rest easily. Family members and acquaintances alike were questioned, but no one suspected Jens. By now, he had fully identified himself with Elizabeth's life and suffering. He *had* to protect her. His life had meaning only so long as hers was preserved.

When in October 1985 the police wanted to question Jens, he and Elizabeth fled to Europe together, then to Asia. They raced from country to country, keeping their heads above water with falsified documents, fraud, and bad checks. The "madness for two" was shared fairly and completely between the two of them.

Jens was utterly immersed in Elizabeth's world. His days as a model student, over-achiever, rising star, scholarship winner, and well-mannered son of a diplomat were long gone. For months, Jens' parents knew nothing of his whereabouts and then read of his arrest in a newspaper in June 1986.

Jens and Elizabeth were apprehended in London for check fraud on April 30, 1986. In their London apartment, police found suspicious letters, strange journal entries, and false Canadian passports. They contacted the authorities in the U.S., learned of the unsolved murder case in Virginia, and the circle was closed.

Jens' world collapsed around him when he was taken into custody and separated from Elizabeth. He asked obsessively about her welfare and was beside himself with concern for her. Again and again, he asked to see a lawyer; but for four days, from June 5 to June 8, 1986, he was interrogated for hours at a time by three detectives without the benefit of legal representation. He had no lawyer, no Elizabeth, no one he could trust. On June 8, the evening before his appearance in court, under pressure, after several fruitless interrogations, intimidated by the police, worried about Elizabeth, without an attorney and without any tape recordings, Jens confessed to the murders exactly as he and Elizabeth had discussed in the early morning hours of March 31, 1985. He believed this to be his last opportunity to keep his promise to Elizabeth, to prove his love, fulfill his duty, and thereby save his honor. He kept his word.

Although Jens played his role well, he wasn't able to answer many questions. He described the scene of the crime incorrectly, was unable to give a correct account of the position of the bodies, described the wrong type of knife used as the murder weapon, and made mistakes in the description of Nancy Haysom's clothing. Elizabeth had neglected to share these details with him, so he had to find halfway credible explanations to fill in the gaps.

During a separate interrogation on June 8, 1986, Elizabeth also briefly confessed to the murders, flippantly saying, "I did it myself . . . I get off on it." She later retracted this admission and claimed that she'd meant to be "facetious." From that point on, Elizabeth maintained that she had instigated the murders and was an accomplice, but that Jens was the perpetrator. Jens repeated his false confession later in the presence of a German attorney in the hope that he'd be handed over to Germany and thereby avoid a trial and the death penalty in the U.S. His reenactment of *Macbeth* had gotten completely out of control.

At one point, Elizabeth reacted angrily when the detectives seized upon her own words and referred to her as "Lady Macbeth" and Jens as a "poor boy."

A thorough examination, conducted by a forensic psychiatrist in London, concluded that Elizabeth suffered from borderline personality disorder and was a pathological liar. The disorder can manifest itself in, among other things: delusions, persecution mania, impulsiveness, loss of moral inhibitions, fear of abandonment, identity crisis, drug abuse, symptoms of narcissism, extreme idealization or devaluation, and a strong need to control others. Other indicators are: difficulties with forming relationships, unstable but intense relationships, manipulation of other people, and a sense of entitlement.

With Jens, the diagnosis was induced psychosis or shared psychotic disorder. In this illness, a healthy person is taken over by the delusions of the mentally ill partner: the same insanity, the same delusional system, and the same value system are shared by the two people. This is followed by a loss of individual identity, a withdrawal from what is perceived to be a hostile environment, and increasing social isolation. The shared delusion creates a bond. According to the London psychiatrist's court report, "Miss Haysom had a stupefying and mesmeric effect on Soering, which led to an abnormal psychological state in which he became unable to think rationally or question the absurdities in Miss Haysom's view of her life."

After separation, the symptoms of delusion vanish quite rapidly from the affected person. So it was with Jens, as well. Little by little, he realized through his conversations with psychiatrists how gullible, unstable, and impressionable he had been, and how unreal the relationship had been. He slowly awoke from his trance.

Elizabeth wasn't pleased when she noticed that Jens had freed himself from her influence, that he'd slipped away from her, that the tone of his letters had changed, and that his judgment and critical faculties had returned. In 1987, she wrote one last bitter letter, terminating her friendship and accusing him of high treason.

She agreed to cooperate with the prosecuting attorney in Virginia by testifying in court against Jens. After her extradition to the U.S. in 1987, she pleaded guilty to instigating the murders and was sentenced to 90 years in prison. She admitted to wanting her parents killed, but disputed being at the scene of the murders. The judge, as well as two of Elizabeth's brothers, spoke against her early release on parole due to the severity of the crimes.

In the meantime, Jens continued to fight his extradition to the U.S. He retracted his false confession, and barely avoided the death penalty by appealing to the European Court of Human Rights. In June 1990, after years of uncertainty, he appeared in court in Bedford, Virginia.

The trial was a long-anticipated and much-advertised media

spectacle in Virginia—the first local trial to be broadcast on television. In front of the courthouse, a tabloid hack sold copies of a sensationalistic, exploitative book about Jens and Elizabeth—and made a fortune. Bedford's prosecuting attorney had waited four long years for Jens' extradition.

The judge was a friend of the Haysom family and had gone to school with Nancy Haysom's brother. For four years, the whole town had been exposed to TV and newspaper reports that had portrayed Jens as a monster for whom murder was merely a mathematical problem, a mere game.

The Soering family was absolutely convinced of Jens' innocence and retained a well-known attorney from Detroit. He proved to be incompetent; in 1993 he lost his license due to psychological problems and professional negligence (as well as misappropriation of funds and mishandling cases). Yet this attorney had been recommended to the Soering family as an outstanding lawyer and expert.

Elizabeth became a witness for the prosecution and took the stand to lay the blame on Jens. The prosecuting attorney feared Jens' oft-discussed IQ and seemed to want to compete with him in regard to intelligence, eloquence, and sarcasm. By contrast, Jens often seemed unsure of himself and smiled nervously.

Jens pled not guilty and testified that he'd taken the blame for the crimes out of love, to deflect suspicion away from Elizabeth and protect her from the death penalty. He was stunned that no one called into question his false confession. Apparently nobody doubted the credibility of Elizabeth's statement, and no one tried to examine her account's inconsistencies. Jens answered questions in a condescending and lecturing manner, often appearing to be arrogant and presumptuous. He did not endear himself to his listeners.

*   *   *

The forensic evidence was very thin.

At the scene of the crime police found, among other things: a smudged, bloody sock print; a bloody sneaker print; a shoeprint in front of the house; type-B blood on a damp cloth in the kitchen; type-O blood in a bedroom; Elizabeth's fingerprints on a vodka bottle; an unidentified hair; and an unidentified fingerprint on a shot glass. Jens has blood type O, which is shared by roughly 45 percent of the population. Elizabeth has blood type B, as does approximately 10 percent of the population. Both the O type and the B type blood from the crime scene were destroyed during testing.

The Haysoms had been drinking and were obviously not surprised by an intruder. After dinner they had drinks and ice cream with someone they knew. There was no trace of Jens at the scene. There were no fingerprints belonging to him, no hair, no testable DNA, and no eyewitnesses. The sneaker print was smaller than his shoe size.

Significant details of the crime scene did not match with Jens' description. Judging by the evidence at the crime scene, two people were with the Haysoms—suggesting two perpetrators. The knife that Jens described as the murder weapon was not the type of knife used. Jens later said that he'd learned of many of the details at the trial, and that he'd never seen the crime scene itself.

According to Elizabeth's testimony, the motive for the crime was that her parents objected to her relationship with Jens. This motive seems implausible, and there's no supporting evidence for it. In her numerous letters, Elizabeth never mentioned that her parents didn't like Jens, that they didn't approve of the relationship, or that they wanted to put an end to it. A reporter who followed the case and the entire trial later said that he'd never believed this motive. In addition, such a weak motive does not sufficiently explain the brutal manner in which the murders were carried out: both Haysoms were found with their throats cut through to the bone.

Elizabeth exhibited a tendency for vague, evasive, rambling answers. At her trial in 1987, she went on record with so many different, contradictory, and tangled versions of reasons and events that the prosecuting attorney eventually became unnerved and worn down. Still, it was easier to attribute such a crime to the cool, efficient German than to the Haysom's own daughter.

Lacking any concrete evidence, the entirety of the prosecution's argument against Jens rested on two things: Jens' recanted confession and the smudged, bloody sock print found at the scene of the crime. The prosecuting attorney compared the sock print to Jens' footprint and triumphantly declared that it "fits like a glove."

Unlike a fingerprint, a sock print is in no way a precise, empirical piece of evidence. Because sock prints are inexact and possess no ridges, they don't lend themselves to clear, doubt-free attribution. But Jens' attorney waited until after the trial, when it was too late, to compare the sock print to Elizabeth's footprint—and found that it matched as well as Jens'. After the trial, one of the jury members said in an interview that at first he believed Jens to be innocent; only the sock print persuaded him to vote "guilty."

Jens was found guilty and sentenced to two life terms in prison.

Many important questions were ignored during the presentation of the case, and they remain unanswered even today. Whose fingerprint was on the glass next to Derek Haysom? Who was the second person at the crime scene? Who left the sneaker print? It's unlikely that one single perpetrator could have killed both victims at the same time. The struggle apparently began in the dining room and spread out from there: Nancy Haysom was found in the kitchen, and Derek Haysom was found in the living room.

Someone had obviously tried to get rid of evidence after committing the crime. The floor was wiped, as were objects. While cleaning up her parents' house in the summer of 1985 with her half-siblings and friends, a neighbor observed Elizabeth as she took off a shoe and compared her foot with a sock print on the floor. The neighbor found this strange and reported it to the police department.

Elizabeth appropriated the only alibi for herself in court in 1990. Even though she maintained that *she* had gone to see two movies in D.C., she could not correctly identify the movies' starting times on the ticket. The mileage on the rental car showed that someone had driven many miles more than the distance between Washington, D.C. and Lynchburg. Whoever bought the tickets at the time the crime was committed cannot have been at the scene of the crime.

The victims suffered deep neck wounds as well as numerous superficial stab wounds. The repetition and shallowness of the latter suggest that they were committed by someone who was mentally ill and/or physically weak—or possibly under the influence of drugs. Jens did not abuse drugs, and never experimented with them. As of March 30, 1985, he'd never exhibited any psychological problems.

In her countless tall tales, Elizabeth had always portrayed her parents as exceedingly wealthy, but also stingy. She constantly quarreled with them about spending money and felt crushed by their control over her. In court, she testified that on the weekend of March 23, 1985—one week before the murders—she'd stolen a piece of jewelry from her mother in order to finance a heroin buy. At the crime scene the police found an open drawer and a necklace lying on the floor in Elizabeth's room. It is quite unlikely that the drawer was left open between March 23 and 30, that the necklace was left lying on the floor for an entire week and never picked up. Could it be that an argument broke out on the night of the crime over the piece of jewelry stolen a week earlier?

The Haysom's wealth was widely overestimated; their social standing was greater by far than their actual worth. When the estate was probated, the only significant assets were their small house and two automobiles.

A week after the crime, in April 1985, two suspicious vagabonds were apprehended in the Lynchburg area. The evidence at the crime scene indicated that there was no forced entry or robbery. Whoever entered the house must have been sufficiently known to and trusted by the Haysoms that they allowed this person to wander through the house in socks and to sit down at the dinner table with them.

The Haysoms barely knew Jens, and it's improbable that they would have allowed him into the house alone, without Elizabeth. Nor is it likely that they would have asked him in, especially at night after dinner, without being invited or announced. If someone had truly intended to commit murder, why would they have taken off their shoes at the front door when this would have only made a later escape more difficult?

In a TV interview, one of Elizabeth's half-brothers later said that she'd always lied and that he believed she was present at the scene of the crime. His parents had certainly not invited Jens into the house without Elizabeth. Judging by the crime scene and especially the type of injuries, hatred was involved in the motive, which suggests a close relationship existed between perpetrator and victim.

*   *   *

For many there still remain justified doubts over the conviction of Jens Soering.

Gail Marshall, a former deputy attorney general of Virginia, is absolutely certain that Jens would be free today if he'd had a better lawyer. She speaks of a "moral certitude" that Jens cannot be the perpetrator. She is convinced that procedural error led to a wrongful conviction. According to Marshall, "Confessions are sometimes false, and juries sometimes make mistakes." In her long professional career, she has only had two cases come across her desk in which there was obviously a wrongful conviction: Earl Washington, Jr. and Jens Soering. Earl Washington, Jr. had also falsely confessed to a crime that he didn't commit. In contrast to Jens' case, Washington's innocence was later proved through the use of DNA.

Gail Marshall was so certain that Jens was unjustly convicted that she took over his habeas corpus proceedings in 1995. However, in 2001, without any hearing being granted, the U.S. Supreme Court denied all appeals and attempts to reopen the case.

That year, Jens finally collapsed under the pressure. His mother had died in 1997 and he blamed himself for her early death. His last appeal having been denied, all hope for legal redress was gone. Jens was left completely alone, without hope for justice. For fifteen long years, he'd waited for a review of his case, in the hope of finally being vindicated.

Jens thought about suicide, but instead dared to make a new beginning. He started from rock bottom, began to meditate regularly, and started writing a book in order to make something positive out of his life. *The Way of the Prisoner* was published by Lantern Books in 2003. Since then, Jens spends two hours every day in contemplative prayer, is a professed Christian, has had a total of five books published (as well as three translations), maintains contact with countless advocates and supporters, and leads a meditation group and a Tai Chi group in the prison.

He dreams of one day being allowed to visit the grave of his mother, of seeing Germany with his own eyes, of living in a monastery, and of never again in his life having to speak English.

His attorneys and some supporters are active advocates for him, and a few journalists cannot let go of the Soering case. If things happened the way Jens says they happened, then he is unjustly in prison for life. He tells his story unwaveringly; his version has not changed since 1990. Jens has a spotless prison record and has not received a single disciplinary charge over the years. Most who speak with Jens are surprised by his frankness. He willingly answers all questions, makes no excuses for himself, and is discerning and alert. Jens is a sympathetic person, an exceptionally intelligent conversationalist, and an attentive listener.

The fact that he asserts over and over that he did not participate in the crime is a real disadvantage for him when it comes to the Virginia Parole Board: denial of guilt is interpreted as lack of remorse, and remorse is a necessary requirement for clemency or release. As long as he claims he did not commit the crime, he will never be released.

This is admittedly only one side of the story. We don't know what the other side is.

Today Elizabeth Haysom finds herself at a women's correctional center in Fluvanna, Virginia. She has never again spoken of the case and declines all interviews. No one knows how she feels today, if she has changed, if she can remember the past, if she even thinks about it, or if she's suppressed it or reimagined it to fit her situation.

The second person who was probably also at the scene of the crime has never been found. This person could possibly confirm that Elizabeth was present.

While Elizabeth is silent, she does not lack admirers. One author who intended to write a crime story about her had to hand off the project to a colleague because he'd fallen completely and hopelessly in love with her. Jens has not seen or spoken with Elizabeth since 1990; her last letter to him was written in 1987. He doesn't ever want to see her again.

The lives of the Haysoms are irretrievably lost. Who was actually in the Haysom house at the time of the crime is unclear. Jens and Elizabeth describe different versions of the course of events. Essentially, it's his word against hers. One of the two was in Washington, D.C. at the time of the crime, watching movies in a theater; one of the two is telling the truth. There remain countless unanswered questions, and there is the possibility that the actual perpetrator remains at large.

Perhaps the central question is no longer what exactly happened those many years ago, but rather what should happen now.

The likelihood that Elizabeth will one day clear Jens is vanishingly small. She has already applied several times for early release on parole. The official end of her sentence is May 2032.

Jens does not have an official end to his sentence. A life sentence in Virginia means until death. Jens was 19 years old when he went to prison.

POSTSCRIPT

When Patricia McGinty wrote the afterword for the German edition of this book, which was published in 2008, there seemed to be no prospect for change in either my living conditions or my legal situation—let alone the case evidence. But the next few years turned out to be the most tumultuous of my life.

On September 22, 2009, I was transferred from Brunswick Correctional Center in Lawrenceville, Virginia, to Buckingham Correctional Center in Dillwyn, Virginia, because Brunswick was slated for closure. Its per capita operational costs were the highest of any prison in Virginia and the state's budget crisis was now so severe that even the Department of Corrctions had to sacrifice one of its facilities.

Like Brunswick, Buckingham is a level-three, medium-security penitentiary housing 1,100 comparatively well-behaved inmates of all ages, from their late teens to their seventies. Some are only serving short sentences for non-violent crimes, but were transferred here because they got into fights at low-security facilities. And some are serving life without parole for rape-murders or, in one case, hijacking an airliner in the 1970s.

Unlike Brunswick, there is far more gang activity at Buckingham, though serious fights and rapes are still relatively rare. Or perhaps they are simply not reported: two nights before I wrote these lines, a prisoner was beaten to a bloody pulp over a

161

single first-class (44 cent) stamp. Apparently, the guards didn't notice.

Buckingham offers far fewer classes and activities than Brunswick did—no Tai Chi or centering prayer groups here!— perhaps because a less enriched lifestyle is cheaper. At the end of the day, money really is *the* determining factor in corrections. This principle applies to the convicts as well, of course: the inmate gambling operations at Buckingham are the most sophisticated I have ever seen in my twenty-five-year career in the penitentiary.

Although I participated in prison life at Brunswick through various activities of a religious or literary nature, I have kept to myself since my arrival at Buckingham. The reason for my withdrawal is simple: lack of time. Almost as soon as I arrived at the facility, I was swept up by a series of events that requested my full and constant attention, mostly in the form of writing hundreds of letters to my supporters in the U.S. and Germany.

On September 24, 2009, the Virginia Department of Forensic Sciences released the results of DNA tests performed on 42 biological samples found in the Haysom murder case file from 1985. Thirty-one of the samples yielded no useable results because the material was too degraded or too minute. But the other 11 samples were tested successfully, and turned out to belong neither to me nor Elizabeth Haysom. Unfortunately, these 11 samples could not be matched to any genetic profile in Virginia's DNA Data Bank, so the person who left these blood spatters at the crime scene remains unknown.

A little over three weeks later, on October 19, 2009, Virginia's outgoing governor Timothy M. Kaine met with my supporters and verbally agreed to repatriate me to Germany— if that country could guarantee that I'd spend a significant period of time in a German prison. (A repatriation is essentially an international prison transfer, which allows foreign inmates to serve their sentences in their own countries instead of abroad.)

On January 12, 2010, after receiving assurances that I would be incarcerated in Germany for at least another two years, Governor Kaine officially asked U.S. Attorney General Eric H. Holder to repatriate me.

Precisely one week later, on his first working day in office, Virginia's newly installed Republican governor Robert F. McDonnell withdrew his Democratic predecessor's request for my repatriation. This was the first occasion in Virginia's 234-year history that a governor had reversed his predecessor's decision in an individual case retroactively.

Over the following months, a state senator who represented Lynchburg in Virginia's general assembly mounted a campaign to put political pressure on Attorney General Holder. At one point the general assembly passed a unanimous (92 to 0) resolution demanding that my repatriation be stopped—another first in the history of the commonwealth.

On July 6, 2010, Attorney General Holder announced that he wouldn't repatriate me until a Virginia court ruled whether in fact Governor McDonnell had the legal authority to overrule Governor Kaine's decision. On January 18, 2011, one of my attorneys, Steven D. Rosenfield, submitted a "declaratory judgment" lawsuit seeking judicial clarification of this point of law. The next day, my other attorney, Gail A. Ball, submitted a petition to Governor McDonnell asking him to support my parole application and deportation to Germany, based on the DNA test results. Until that point, Governor McDonnell hadn't been aware of the DNA tests.

Over the following weeks, the Virginia and German media went into a feeding frenzy over this startling development in my case. On March 1, the *Lynchburg News and Advance*—the same newspaper that one year earlier had campaigned to stop my repatriation—even published a column calling for my return home.

On March 21, attorney Ball submitted another petition to Governor McDonnell containing the affidavit and videotaped deposition of Tony Buchanan, a Bedford County resident who'd owned and operated a car transmission repair shop locally for many years. Mr. Buchanan testified that shortly after the murders in 1985, a Chevrolet was delivered to his shop to be repaired. It was picked up and paid for by Elizabeth Haysom (he had no doubt about that) and a young man who was definitely *not* me (he was completely sure about that, too). In the footwell on the driver's side of the car was a puddle of dried blood and a blood-stained hunting knife. Mr. Buchanan thought the young couple might have been hunting deer out of season and thus he didn't report the matter to police.

After the Virginia and German media entered a second feeding frenzy based on Mr. Buchanan's testimony, Governor McDonnell gave a TV interview in Lynchburg on March 30, in which he emphasized the independence of the new parole board, which he'd recently appointed. He pointed out that I had been eligible for parole for years.

Six days later, on April 5, 2011, former governor Kaine announced that he would seek the Democratic Party's nomination for the U.S. Senate seat being vacated by Democrat Jim Webb at the 2012 elections. His likely opponent was Republican former governor George F. Allen, whose main claim to fame was the abolition of parole for all defendants convicted after 1995. (Parole still exists, at least in theory, for defendants like me, who were convicted before 1995.)

Over the following weeks, more than two dozen articles appeared in the press in which Republican spokesmen attacked former governor Kaine as "soft on crime" for his decision to seek my repatriation in 2010.

On May 24, 2011, Governor McDonnell released a strongly

worded statement expressing his faith in my conviction despite the DNA test results and Mr. Buchanan's testimony. Governor McDonnell reaffirmed his belief that I should serve my sentence in a Virginia prison, and he refused to support my parole—after I had spent, at that point, 25 years in prison.

On July 24, the Virginia Parole Board denied my request for release for the seventh time. In addition to citing the "serious nature and circumstances of the offense," as it had done in previous years, the board offered another reason: "risk to the community." This extra reason was cited even though, if granted parole, I would automatically have been deported to Germany.

At the time of the publication of this American version of *One Day in the Life of 179212*, that is where my case rests.

NOTES

1 Adam Liptak, "To More Inmates, Life Term Means Dying Behind Bars," *New York Times*, October 2, 2005; Adam Liptak, "Jailed for Life After Crimes as Teenagers," *New York Times*, October 3, 2005.

2 On November 8, 2006, Virginia had 31,623 inmates in prison and 29,337 in jail. However, roughly three and a half thousand of the inmates in jail actually belonged in prison, which is why Virginia had a "prison population" of approximately 35,000. Report by Sterling C. Proffit, Virginia Board of Corrections Minutes, November 15, 2006, p. 4.

3 Roy Walmsley, *World Prison Population List*, 6th ed. (London: Home Office Research, Development and Statistics Directorate, 2006), see www.prisonstudies.org (International Centre for Prison Studies).

4 William J. Sabol, Heather Couture, and Paige M. Harrison, *Prisoners in 2006* (Washington, D.C.: Bureau of Justice Statistics, 2007), p. 4.

5 Walmsley, *World Prison*, op. cit.

6 C. J. Mumola, *Veterans in Prison or Jail* (Washington, D.C.: Bureau of Justice Statistics, 2000).

7 Kristen A. Hughes, *Justice Expenditures and Employment in the United States* (Washington, D.C.: Bureau of Justice Statistics, 2003); Frank Green, "VA's Prison Population Forecast to Rise," *Richmond Times-Dispatch*, January 7, 2008.

8 Sabol, Couture, and Harrison, *Prisoners in 2006*, op. cit.

9 R. Hawthorne, FOM#B, BWCC, and Rev. William Twine, Onesimus House, both told me that all three daily meals together cost less than $2. The precise figure of $1.83 comes from the neighboring state of Maryland: Eric Rich, "For Victims, a Glimpse of Life Behind Prison Gates," *Washington Post*, April 21, 2004.

10 Patrick A. Langan and David J. Levin, *Recidivism of Prisoners Released in 1994*, (Washington, D.C.: Bureau of Justice Statistics, June 2002).

11 Frank Green, "Cellmate Charged in Killing of Ausley," *Richmond Times-Dispatch*, June 4, 2004.

12 Wendy Koch, "Despite High-profile Cases, Sex Offense Crimes Decline," *USA Today*, August 25, 2005.

13 According to a study of seven states in 2000 by Ohio University. Jayne O'Donnell, "State Time or Federal Prison?" *USA Today*, March 18, 2004. Other studies came to the same result: see Jens Soering, *The*

Convict Christ: What the Gospel Says About Criminal Justice, (Maryknoll, N.Y.: Orbis Books, 2006).

14 Allen J. Beck and Timothy A. Hughes, *Sexual Violence Reported by Correctional Authorities, 2004* (Washington, D.C.: Bureau of Justice Statistics, July 2005), p. 2.

15 Michael M. Horrock, "Hundreds of Thousands Raped in US Lockups," United Press International, July 31, 2002.

16 Other inmates broke my hand twice—in 1986 and 1989—while playing soccer. However, these incidents may have been accidents.

17 Sabol, Couture, and Harrison, *Prisoners in 2006,* op. cit.

18 Frank Green, "Banned Items a Big Issue at Prison," *Richmond Times-Dispatch,* March 19, 2007.

19 Michelle Groenke, "Prison Chief Admits Kickback Scheme," UPI, July 6, 2006.

20 Bill Sizemore, "Prisoners' Calls Prove Revenue Boon for Virginia," *Virginian Pilot,* February 1, 2004; Bill Sizemore, "Whatever Happened to . . . the Prepaid Prison Telephone System?" *Virginian Pilot,* March 6, 2006.

21 Dan Ackerman, "Bernie Ebbers Guilty," *Forbes Magazine,* March 15, 2005.

22 C. G. Camp and G. M. Camp, *The 2000 Corrections Yearbook: Adult Corrections* (Middletown, Conn.: Criminal Justice Institute, 2000), p. 54.

23 B. Jaye Anno, Camelia Graham, James E. Lawrence, and Ronald Shansky, *Correctional Health Care—Addressing the Needs of Elderly, Chronically Ill, and Terminally Ill Inmates* (Washington, D.C.: Department of Justice / National Institute of Corrections, February 2004), p. 9; see www.ncic.org.

24 "California Struggling with Growing Numbers of Elderly Prisoners," Associated Press, June 9, 2002.

25 Marc Mauer, Ryan S. King, and Malcolm C. Young, *The Meaning of "Life": Long Prison Sentences in Context* (Washington, D.C.: The Sentencing Project, 2004), p. 25.

26 Paul von Zielbauer, "Private Health Care in Jails Can Be a Death Sentence," *New York Times,* February 27, 2005. See also John E. Dannenberg, "PHS Redux: Sued in a Dozen States, Contract Losses, Stock Plummets, Business Continues," *Prison Legal News,* November 2006, pp. 1–10.

27 Connie Cass, "Prison Population Grew 2.9 percent in 2003," Associated Press, May 28, 2004.

28 *Prevalence of Imprisonment in the U.S. Population, 1974–2001* (Washington, D.C.: Bureau of Justice Statistics, August 2003).

29 Eric Lottke, *Hobbling a Generation* (Baltimore: National Center on Institutions and Alternatives, 1997).

30 Richard Morin, "Answer to AIDS Mystery Found Behind Bars," *Washington Post,* March 9, 2006.

31 Fox Butterfield, "With Longer Sentences, Cost of Fighting Crime Is Higher," *New York Times,* May 3, 2004; John J. Gibbons and Nicholas

de B. Katzenbach, eds., *Confronting Confinement: A Report of the Commission on Safety and Abuse in America's Prisons* (New York: Vera Institute, 2006), p. 6.

32 Marvin Mentor, "California Corrections System Declared Dysfunctional—Redemption Doubtful," *Prison Legal News*, March 2005, pp. 1, 5; see Corrections Independent Review Panel (CIRP), *Reforming Corrections*, June 30, 2004; Marvin Mentor, "Pay to Play: Guard Union Spreads the Wealth," *Prison Legal News*, March 2005, p. 5.; John Pomfret, "California's Crisis in Prison System a Threat to Public," *Washington Post*, June 11, 2006.

33 Christina Nuckols, "Prison Supporters Rally," *Virginian Pilot*, August 30, 2002.

34 Ibid.

35 Joanne Mariner, *No Escape: Male Rape in U.S. Prisons* (New York: Human Rights Watch, 2001).

36 Brent Staples, "Fighting the A.I.D.S. Epidemic by Issuing Condoms in the Prisons," *New York Times*, September 7, 2004.

37 Other states report HIV/AIDS infection rates of only 1.9 percent to 2.9 percent. Why the big difference? Because New York tests all of its inmates, whereas other states give tests only to those prisoners who request one. This practice allows other states to reduce medical costs. *HIV in Prison 2001* (Washington, D.C.: Bureau of Justice Statistics, 2004); Brent Staples, "Treat the Epidemic Behind Bars Before It Hits the Streets," *New York Times*, June 22, 2004.

38 Mauer et al., *The Meaning*, op. cit., Langan and Levin, *Recidivism*, op. cit.

39 Anno et al., *Correctional Health*, op. cit, p. 7; Larry O'Dell, Associated Press, "10 Years Later: Abolition of Parole Has Not Created a Building Frenzy," *Virginian Pilot*, January 3, 2005.

40 In the first six months of 2006, the Virginia Parole Board reviewed 2,130 male prisoners' cases, denied parole in 2,069 cases, and granted parole in 61. Virginia Department of Corrections/Virginia Parole Board Website for January to June 2006.

41 Education as Crime Prevention, O.S.I. Criminal Justice Initiative, September 1997.

42 Caroline Wolf Harlow, *Education and Correctional Populations* (Washington, D.C.: Bureau of Justice Statistics, 2003), p. 1, 3.

43 Samantha M. Shapiro, "Jails for Jesus," *Mother Jones*, November/December 2003; Brigitte Sarabi, "Sentencing Policy in the 21st Century," *Justice Matters* (Western Prison Project), Winter 2005, pp. 11–12; Nancy G. La Vigne et al., *A Portrait of Prisoner Reentry* (Washington, D.C.: Urban Institute, 2003).

44 Alan Elsner, "Inmates 'Do Not Pass Go' Card," *Los Angeles Times*, January 29, 2004.

45 Joe Eaton, "Prisoners, Pups Embrace through Program," *Virginian Pilot*, December 5, 2005.

46 First Place—Best Book on Social Concerns—2007 Catholic Press Association Awards. See *The Catholic Journalist*, Vol. 59, Nr. 6, June 2007.

47 Adam Liptak, "Study Suspects Thousands of False Convictions," *New York Times*, April 19, 2004.

48 Robert S. Mueller III, *Preliminary Semiannual Uniform Crime Report, January through June 2006* (Washington, D.C.: Federal Bureau of Investigations, December 18, 2006); Kathleen Kingsbury, "The Next Crime Wave," *Time*, December 11, 2006.

49 Marc Mauer, *Race to Incarcerate* (New York: The New Press, 1999), pp. 82–84; Richard Willing, "Inmate Population Rises as Crime Drops," *USA Today*, July 29, 2003; Connie Cass, "Prison Population Grows by 2.9 percent in 2003," Associated Press, May 29, 2004; Richard Willing, "US Prison Populations on the Rise," *USA Today*, May 28, 2004; *Report of the Re-entry Policy Council* (Washington, D.C.: Council of State Governments/Urban Institute Re-entry Policy Forum, February 2005), p. xvii citing Paige M. Harrison and Allen J. Beck, *Prisoners in 2003* (Washington, D.C.: Bureau of Justice Statistics, 2004); Walmsley, *World Prison*, op. cit.

50 Curt Anderson, "Violent Crime Rate for 2003 Holds Steady," Associated Press, September 13, 2004; "2004 Crime Rate Hovered at Low Levels," *USA Today*, September 26, 2005.

51 In 2006 there were 1,417,145 violent crimes—an increase of 21,050 over 2005—and 9,983,568 non-violent offenses—a decrease of 182,591. Therefore, there was a net reduction of 155,541 crimes of all kinds from 2005 to 2006. See Robert S. Mueller III, *Crime in the United States, 2006* (Washington, D.C.: Federal Bureau of Investigations, September 24th, 2007). See also Howard N. Snyder, "Not This Time: A Response to the Warnings of the Juvenile Superpredator," *Corrections Today*, April 2007, p. 116.

52 *Encyclopedia Britannica—Micropedia Vol. 9*, (Chicago: Encyclopedia Britannica, Inc., 1988), p. 710; Thomas P. O'Connor, "What Works, Religion as a Correctional Intervention: Part 1," *Journal of Community Corrections*, Vol. XIV, Nr. 1, Fall 2004, p. 20, citing J. McGuire, "Evidence-based Programming Today," paper presented at the International Community Corrections Association Annual Conference in Boston, Mass., 2002.

53 *Card v. D.C. Dept. of Corr.*, USD.C. ED VA, Case No. 2:00-vc-00631JBF.

54 Kevin Johnson, "After Years in Solitary, Freedom Hard to Grasp," *USA Today*, June 9, 2005.

55 Michael Rigby, "Report Lambastes New York Lockdowns," *Prison Legal News*, February 2005, p. 9.

56 Frank Green, "Prisons Segregate Rastafarians," *Richmond Times-Dispatch*, September 17, 2005.

57 Letter from Rev. Ronald J. Sider to Jens Soering, May 17, 2007.

58 Adam Liptak, "Locked Away Forever After Crimes as Teenagers," *New York Times*, October 3, 2005.

59 Chris Suellentrop, "The Right Has a Jailhouse Conversion," *New York Times*, December 24, 2006.

60 On August 28, 2006, and March 28, 2007.

61 Michael Hardy, "ACLU: Prison Care Lacking," *Richmond Times-Dispatch*, May 8, 2003.

62 Staples, "Treat," op. cit.; Will S. Hylton, "Sick on the Inside: Correctional HMO's and the Coming Prison Plague," *Harper's Magazine*, August 2003.

63 Martha Mendoza, "Imprisoned and Infected," Associated Press/*Milwaukee Journal Sentinel*, April 23, 2007.

64 Marvin Mentor, "Federal Court Seizes California Prisons' Medical Care; Appoints Receiver with Unprecedented Powers," *Prison Legal News*, March 2006, p. 6; see also Andy Furillo, "Receiver Rips Prison-reform Obstructions," *Sacramento Bee*, December 6, 2006.

65 Calculation based on Hardy, "ACLU," op. cit.

66 Green, "Va's Prison Population," op. cit.

67 John E. Dannenberg, "New York HCV Treatment Suit Not Mooted by Equivocal DOC Concession; Class Certification Granted," *Prison Legal News*, March 2007, p. 33.

68 Hylton, "Sick," op. cit.

69 Von Zielbauer, "Private," op. cit.

70 Etienne Benson, "Rehabilitate or Punish?" *Monitor on Psychology* (American Psychological Association), Vol. 34, No.7, July–August 2003, p. 47; see also Anna Bailey, "More Police Means Strain on Corrections System," *The Examiner* (Washington, D.C.), April 17, 2006; and Kevin Johnson, "Commission Warns of Harm Isolation Can Do to Prisoners," *USA Today*, June 8, 2006.

71 Dan Malone, "Cruel and Inhumane," *Amnesty International*, Fall 2005, p. 23.

72 Pete Earley, "Living with Mental Illness," *USA Today*, May 2, 2006.

73 Christopher J. Mumola, *Substance Abuse and Treatment, State and Federal Prisons, 1997*, (Washington, D.C.: Bureau of Justice Statistics, 1997), p. 1. These figures are for state-sentenced prisoners only.

74 *Policy Brief Offender Reentry*, National Association of State Alcohol and Drug Abuse Directors (Washington, D.C.), p. 1; see also Kevin Knight, D. Dwayne Simpson, and Matthew Miller, "Three-Year Re-Incarceration Outcomes for In-Prison Therapeutic Community Treatment in Texas," *Prison Journal*, Vol. 79, 1999, pp. 337–351.

75 "Study Shows Prison-Based Treatment Benefits Everyone," *Justice Matters* (Western Prison Project), Spring 2005, p. 8.

76 Mumola, *Substance Abuse*, op. cit., p. 8.

77 Howard N. Snyder and Melissa Sickmund, *Juvenile Offenders and Victims: 2006 National Report* (Washington, D.C.: U.S. Department of Justice, 2006), pp. 236, 237. Earley, op. cit.

78 Marian Wright Edelman, ed., *The Status of America's Children 2004* (Washington, D.C.: Children's Defense Fund, 2004), p. 151.

ABOUT THE PUBLISHER

LANTERN BOOKS was founded in 1999 on the principle of living with a greater depth and commitment to the preservation of the natural world. In addition to publishing books on animal advocacy, vegetarianism, religion, and environmentalism, Lantern is dedicated to printing books in the U.S. on recycled paper and saving resources in day-to-day operations. Lantern is honored to be a recipient of the highest standard in environmentally responsible publishing from the Green Press Initiative.

www.lanternbooks.com

2011